Islam and Qur'an

~An Introduction~

MURAD HOFMANN

amana publications

Copyright © 2007 amana publications
10710 Tucker Street, Beltsville, Maryland 20705-2223
Tel: (301) 595-5777, Fax: (301) 595-5888, E-mail: amana@igprinting.com

First Edition 1428AH/2007AC
Printed in the United States of America by International Graphics
10710 Tucker Street, Beltsville, Maryland 20705-2223

Library of Congress Cataloging-in-Publicationn Data

Hofmann, Murad Wilfried.
    Islam and Qur'an : an introduction / Murad Wilfried Hofmann.
        p. cm.
    Includes bibliographical references.
    ISBN-13: 978-1-59008-047-4
    1. Islam--Essence, genius, nature. 2. Islam--Doctrines. 3. Koran--Criticism,
interpretation, etc. I. Title.
    BP163.H642 2007
    297--dc22

    2007015610

CONTENTS

PART TWO: AN INTRODUCTION TO THE QUR'AN

– Part One –

An Introduction
to Islam

INTRODUCTION

To seek reliable knowledge about Islam makes particular sense these days because it is the one and only religion currently on the rise. Already 1.4 billion people consider themselves Muslim, and this number is growing by the minute. Muslims are of course no longer found only within the 57 member states of the Organization of the Islamic Conference (O.I.C.). Today there is not a single country world-wide without some Muslim presence.

Western, Southern and Northern Europe in addition to local Muslims now is the home of some 15 million Muslim immigrants, mainly from India, Pakistan, Bangla Desh, Somalia, Turkey, North Africa, Black Africa, Albania, and Bosnia. Thus in Great Britain, France, Germany, Italy, Spain, Sweden and Denmark Islam has become the second religion, after Catholicism or Protestantism. Already, we find four Muslims in the British House of Lords...

At the same time, the Islamic populations traditional in Eastern Europe—Albanians, Bosnians, Chechenians and Tatars—have all gone through a vitalizing process of re-Islamization.

In the United States as well, in spite of the tragic events of 9/11, Islam continues to grow almost dramatically. Its extraordinary dynamics are due both to the religious fervor of Afro-American Muslims (37,5%) and the extremely high percentage of Muslim academics, mostly immigrants of Indo-Pakistani and Arabic stock. In regional centers of Islam like Los Angeles, Detroit, Chicago, New York, and Washington, D.C. one out of five medical doctors now is Muslim. In America, the number of mosques doubled to more than 1250 since 1990. By 2010 the Muslim community in the U.S. might reach 10 million, i.e. 3% of the total population.

American Muslims pride themselves on the first Muslim Nobel Prize winner in natural sciences, Dr. Ferid Murad (1998). Just as they are proud of the fact that Muslim computer specialists had made essential contributions to the development of the INTEL Pentium III processor. They consider themselves as the last defenders of the moral values originally held by the Founding Fathers of the American Federation. And, as suggested by a book called "The Sun rises in the West", they expect the necessary rejuvenation of the Muslim Orient to be inspired by the Muslim Occident.

Reason enough for everyone to make the effort of learning substantially more about Islam as a religion and civilization. To understand Muslims—their beliefs and expectations—has never been more important than today, in the interest of peace both at home and in the international arena. After all, as put by Johannes Rau, former German Federal President, we should "live with, and not against, each other".

Every true religion is characterized by (i) a universal world view, (ii) ritualized forms of communication with the Divine, (iii) ethical rules and (iv) religious institutions and symbols. The same is true of Islam, a religion which for 1400 years has served as a key to the understanding of Reality and for living in harmony with it.

And yet, in view of the diversity and pluralism of this religion, one might doubt whether it is possible at all to write authentically about Islam and Muslims, a community far from being monolithic. Did Islam not mean different things to different people at different times? Are there perhaps as many Islams as there are believers? And which Islam am I to describe: Sunni Islam or Shi'a dogmatism? Sufi mysticism or Wahhabi rigorism?

True, the Islamic world at all times showed, and treasured, diversity. Muslims, too, found themselves fighting each other on doctrinal grounds, even though religious wars European style (and of the magnitude of the 30 Years War 1618-1648) never occurred among them.

However, in spite of the absence of an Islamic Vatican, Muslims through all the ages managed to cling to their utmost essentials: Their belief in the unity of God, His Book, and His Prophet was never challenged from within and acted as an all weather glue that tied the Muslim Ummah together, no matter what.

Thus Islam never went through an identity crisis and, after periods of decline, always found enough internal resources for periodic revival and restoration. Today as well, this religion is clearly showing its classic contours.

This introduction while rich in data is compact in size. It only can help open the door for more substantial roaming, for which suggestions are found under Literature.

Such a short introduction cannot be expected to be exhaustive. But it can be expected to be non-partisan and reliable. I vouch indeed for a description of Islam concomitant with what the large majority of all Muslims identify with.

EDITORIAL NOTE

1. For Qur'anic quotations both Surah and Verse are given, separated by colon. Thus 2: 255 refers to verse 255 of Surat al-Baqara. Unless otherwise indicated, English Qur'an quotations are taken from Muhammad Asad, *The Message of the Qur'an*, Gibraltar: Dar al-Andalus 1980.

2. Whenever a Muslim pronounces the name of a prophet, be it Muhammad, Jesus, or Moses, he adds: "God`s blessing and peace be with him!" (salla`llahu ʾalaihi wa-s-salam). In the text this is indicated by the addenda (s.) after the name of a prophet.

3. In the text, within parentheses, Arabic terms are added frequently in order to allow Muslims to orient themselves. Of course, in many cases in English there is no true synonym for an Arabic theological or legal term.

THE FORMATION OF ISLAM

ISLAM AS A WORLD RELIGION

Proceeding straight on from the Red Fort in New Delhi one runs into no less than five religious buildings, belonging to five different religions: a temple devoted to Jainism, a shrine belonging to Sikhs, a Hindu temple, a mosque, and a Baptist church. Who, then, is to question that human beings are basically religious, man quintessentially being a *homo religiosus*, constitutionally bound to ask fundamental philosophical questions like "Where does everything come from?" "What is the purpose of all this?" "How will everything end?"

The answers given to such truly primitive, i.e. primeval and foundational, questions by wise men and women crystallized as religions. And each of them developed its own particular world view, spirituality, ethics, and rites as well as art with specific aesthetics. In short: Through tying man to GOD (religare in Latin), ultimate Reality and primary uncaused Causality of everything, religions became cultural factors as well; most turned into complex civilizations.

Religions adhered to by hundreds of millions are considered "world religions". Today this is the case with Confucianism, Hinduism, Buddhism, Christianity, and Islam. Given its global dissemination, the Mosaic faith is considered a world religion, too, although the number of Jews is limited to a few million. Islam became a world religion on both counts: Muslims now number 1.4 billion, and as of the 20th century their presence has become universal.

ISLAM AS A MONOTHEISTIC RELIGION

One can divide all religions into two groups: Indo-Germanic ones (called Aryan in India) and others (called non-Aryan in India). The first of these two groups can be divided, in turn, into ancient Indian religions of Vedic origin—like Hinduism and Brahmanism—and into non-Vedic ones—like Buddhism, Jainism, Sikhism and Zoroastrianism.

The non-Indo-Germanic religions can as well be subdivided: into Semitic ones–like Judaism, Christianity, and Islam–and non-Semitic ones–like Confucianism, Taoism, and Shintoism.

What sets the three Semitic world religions apart is their concept of a personal God and the fact that they are basing their religious convictions not on ancient myths or philosophical speculation but on revealed scriptures.

The Far Eastern religions, unfamiliar with a personal concept of God, are supportive of a pantheistic-monistic interpretation of Reality. According to Indian mystical traditions Reality is understood as a cyclical cosmic process or as non-personal polarized energy: Everything *is* God.

In practice, however, Far Eastern religions either tended to degenerate into polytheism (like Hinduism) or non-religious techniques for coping with life (like Buddhism).

In contrast, the Semitic religions are supportive of a dualistic-monotheistic interpretation of Reality: One single God and His creation. In Semitic thought God is understood as a self-conscious, intelligent person, self-subsistent and independent of His creation: Everything *belongs to* God. Judaism, Christanity and Islam, all three, in this order, founded in the Middle East, are the "three monotheis-tic world religions" in as much as they all focus on the ways and means of communicating with God.

Whether the Jewish people arrived at monotheism first and in fully independent fashion is, however, questioned by Egyptologists because during the 18th dynasty Pharaoh Amenhotep IV. (better known as Ikhnaton, husband of Nefertiti) had already introduced, through the worship of Aton, a (short lived) monotheistic cult (1350- 1334 B.CE.).

ISLAM AS IBRAHIMIC RELIGION

The core faith of the three monotheistic religions historically goes back to a common religious ancestor: Abraham (Ibrahim in Arabic) who in the Qur'an (3: 65-68) is called a "Muslim" in the original sense of being "submitted" to God. Abraham according to unchallenged tradition became indeed the first monotheist when realizing that polytheism is quite impossible logically. Abraham also was the first human being understanding God, the One and Only, as an actor in world history.

Muslims feel ontologically connected with all people who believe in God, their common Creator. But their Abrahimic linkage with Jews and Christians, in the Qur'an called *Ahl al-Kitab* (People of the Book), goes far beyond that. Islam is indeed the only existing religion which explicitly incorporates previous scriptural revelations. Thus Islam adopted the supreme traits of the Jewish faith–belief in God's Justice–and of the Christian faith–belief in God's Love.

This being said, Muslims only see their own belief in God's Unity (at-tawhid) as crystal clear and untainted. From an Islamic perspective, the Jewish notion of belonging to a "Chosen People", privileged by God—and that on a biological basis—is incompatible with God's Justice and Compassion for mankind as a whole (5: 18; 62: 6). For Muslims equally unacceptable is the Jewish idea of being partner with God of a bilateral treaty, the so-called Covenant; it clashes with God being the Exalted, Sovereign, Supreme, and Absolute who rewards whom He wills and punishes whom He wills.

In turn, Muslims also reject the Christian concept of God, conditioned as it is by the construct that man, suffering from a Hereditary Sin, was in need of a "Salvation" that could only be won through the sacrifice of God incarnate, i.e. Jesus, His divine son. The idea that a human being —and be it a prophet—could be "consubstantial" with God as adopted as ecclesiastical dogma by the First Ecumenical Council in Nicaea, in 325 CE, is considered by Muslims as mere Gnostic speculation. In its 112th Sura, al-Ihklas, the Qur'an makes short shrift with any notions of incarnation:

(1) Say: "He is the One God:

(2) God the Eternal, the Uncaused Cause of all Being,

(3) He begets not, and neither is He begotten;

(4) and there is nothing that could be compared with Him."

By the same token, Muslims consider the Christian construct of Trinity as a serious modification of the Muslim belief in strict and unadulterated monotheism. The doctrine of the Unity of God (at-tawhid) plays such a central role in Islam that the first part of the (two-part) Muslim declaration of faith (ash-shahada) reads "I give witness that there is no god but God" (*ashhadu an la ilaha illa Allah*).

ISLAM AS A REVEALED RELIGION

The followers of all three monotheistic religions all share the view that man cannot hope to unravel the mysteries of being through mere observation and rational analysis of nature. They are conscious of the fact that our sensual perception does not allow reliable conclusions about non-perceptible reality. Consequently, they all consider manifestations of God as both necessary and, of course, possible.

Muslims are indeed deeply convinced that God, beginning with Adam (20: 122), has sent messengers to all nations (10: 47; 28: 45) in order to instruct them about proper living, His role in the universe, and life after death. Particularly important were the prophets sent to the Children of Israel (Banu Israil; 44: 32).

Muslims distinguish between messengers (ar-rasul; sing.) who, like Moses and Muhammad, receive additional, new guidance and prophets (an-nabi; sing.) whose mission it is to help realize the divine messages already received. Accordingly, every messenger of God is a prophet as well while not all prophets are also messengers. Messengers are indeed highly exceptional. Nevertheless, other "inspired" persons may also receive some divine inspirations (al-ilham; sing.) individually.

A MUSLIM PROPHET

The second part of the Muslim declaration of faith (*ash-shahada*) reads: "And I give witness that Muhammad is God's Messenger" (*wa ashhadu anna Muhammadan ar-rasulu'llah*). This refers to the very prophet announced in the Evangel according to John (John. 14, 16 and 16, 13) who in the Qur'an (33: 40) is called the "seal (al-khatam) of all prophets" and thus of revelation: The very last messenger ever sent by God.

From a Muslim perspective such a final messenger was necessary in order to teach mankind **what they knew not** (2: 151) and to correct the deviations in the Jewish and Christian concepts of God described above, and that with a book saying **"no single thing have We neglected in Our decree"** (6: 38).

This prophet of Islam, Muhammad b. `Abdallah, was born on Monday, 17 June, 569 CE, at Makkah; and he died on Monday, 4 June, 632 CE, in al-Madinah. Data of such precision are given in order to underline that the entire life of this prophet took place in the bright light of history, and it has indeed been recorded in the greatest detail, including the most banal facts. Muhammad is indeed the best documented personality of late antiquity.

What a contrast to the situation of the historical sources of the New Testament. They are so precarious that even Christian theologians find it nearly impossible scientifically to prove the historicity of Jesus. One does know a great deal about how Jesus has been represented all through the ages; but one knows next to nothing reliably about what he himself had meant to present.

ARABIA BEFORE MUHAMMAD

Muhammad was born into a well respected but impoverished patrician family. Orphaned at young age, he grew up with a paternal uncle in Makkah. At that time, Arabia lived in relative obscurity in the shadow of the two dominating Eastern empires, Byzantium and Sassanid Persia.

The Arabs were extremely divided politically but held together culturally. They shared not only customs and common values–treasuring bravery and the honor of the family–but a highly developed and poetic language which began to be written, primitively at first, at that very time.

The different Arab tribes, some sedentary, some nomadic, while often suffering from relationships eternally poisoned by vendetta, did, however, religiously respect four peaceful holy months each year during which caravans could reach the famous market fair at Makkah unmolested. This was the occasion as well for poet competitions, highly formalized poetry being the only highly developed form of art in the peninsula.

But Makkah was not only the Arabs` commercial center. With its open air temple, centered around the Ka´aba, it owned a non-denominational shrine that was dear to everybody for being associated with Abraham, his Arab wife Hajar and his Arab son Ismail.

Even though there were some Jewish and Christian tribes around, the majority of the Arabs were rather unreligiously tempered; in particular they could not conceive of life after death. It was customary to pay some tribute to female goddesses like al-Lat, ´Uzza and Manat and to attribute magic qualities to certain stones and trees. However, many Arabs maintained that all divine dignitaries were themselves subordinate under a supreme deity whom they called al-ilah, later turned into Allah. Significantly, this is a term without gender, neither masculine nor feminine, nor allowing plurality.

During this "time of ignorance" (al-jahiliyyah), even though lower deities were considered to be female, Arab women were virtually without rights. There were no limits to polygamy or the number of concubines. Women could not own property, a fact which excluded them from inheritance as well. But they themselves could be inherited, like chattel. No wonder that bedouins would routinely kill baby girls, for economic reasons, by burying them alive.

MUHAMMAD`S MISSION

Muhammad was analphabetic (7: 158) but so much appreciated by everybody as a serious, honest and reliable fellow (al-amin) that Khadija, a successful business woman 15 years his senior, in 596 CE asked him to marry her. With her, mother of his daughter Fatima, until her death in 619 CE he quietly lived a happy monogamous family life, proving himself in his wife`s import-export firm when travelling as her agent all the way to Syria with commercial caravans.

However, as he was about to terminate the fourth decade of his life, Muhammad started to withdraw more and more frequently in order to contemplate the world and his life in it. In 610 CE when he again collected himself in a cave called Hira, high above Makkah on Jabal an-Nur, Muhammad unexpectedly and under for him frightening circumstances received the first divine revelation. An apparition, identified as the angel Gabriel (Jibril), commanded him–unlettered as he was–to read:

(1) **Read in the name of your Sustainer who has created–**

(2) **created man out of a germ-cell !**

(3) **Read–for your Sustainer is the Most Bountiful One**

(4) **who has taught [man] the use of the pen–**

(5) **taught man what he did not know.**

During the 27th night of Ramadan Muslims world-wide commemorate this epochal event, described as it is in the Qur'an:

(1) **Behold, from on high have We bestowed this on the Night of Destiny.**

(2) **And what could make you conceive what it is, that Night of Destiny ?**

(3) **The Night of Destiny is better than a thousand months:**

(4) **in hosts descend in it the angels, bearing divine inspiration by your Sustainer's leave; from all that may happen**

(5) **does it make secure, until the rise of dawn (96: 1-5).**

Muhammad was puzzled by this event which, after a painful pause lasting for months, repeated itself ever so often. He now understood that God had chosen him to be the recipient of his definite concluding message, not only for his countrymen but for mankind as a whole.

What he transmitted challenged, however, the norms and habits of his native Makkan society fundamentally. No wonder that most of his fellow Makkans first reacted to his story with ridicule and scorn, later with an economic boycott enforced against his entire Hashimite clan, and finally with outright persecution and attempted murder.

In accordance with Semitic tradition, sceptical Makkan citizens repeatedly asked Muhammad to prove his divine mission by working miracles (6: 37; 13: 7). This demand could not easily be brushed aside since Jesus was known for his miracles (3: 49; 5: 110). But Muhammad was informed that God alone causes miracles (al-mujizah) to happen (13: 38; 6: 109) by deviating from His habits, known to us as "natural laws".

Muhammad was quite aware that God would only produce one single legitimating miracle for him: the revelation of the Qur'an, step by step (2: 23). In fact, in the view of Muslims, the inimitability (al-ijaz) of the Qur'an is the very "miracle of accreditation" which the Makkan elite had solicited (10: 38; 17: 88)

The mindset of sceptics being what it is, Muhammad had little to gain by announcing, in 616, six years ahead of time, that the then hopelessly inferior Byzantines would beat the very Persians who just had conquered Damascus (613) and Jerusalem (614).

But then, in 621 CE, the Prophet (s.) lived through a magnificent real vision–his nightly journey from Makkah to Jerusalem (al-isra`) and into heaven (al-miraj). The Qur'anic record of these breathtaking events is self-verifying:

(1)   **This fellow man of yours has not gone astray, nor is he diluted,**
(2)   **and neither does he speak out of his own desire:**
(3)   **that is but inspiration with which he is inspired–**
(4)   **something that a very mighty one has imparted to him:**
(5)   **endowed with surpassing power, who in time manifested himself in his true shape and nature,**
(6)   **appearing in the horizon`s loftiest part,**
(7)   **and then drew near, and came close,**
(8)   **until he was but two bow lengths away, or even nearer**
(9)   **And thus did God reveal unto His servant whatever He deemed right to reveal.**
(10) **The heart did not give the lie to what he saw:**
(11) **will you then, contend with him as to what he saw ?**

(12) And, indeed, he saw him a second time
(13) by the lote tree of the farthest limit,
(14) near to the garden of promise,
(15) with the veiled lote tree veiled in a veil of nameless
      splendor...
(16) The eye did not waver, nor yet did it stray:
(17) truly did he see some of the most profound of his
      Sustainer's symbols (53: 2-18).

This is one of the most impressive accounts of a mystical experience–but to no avail as far as the Makkan elite was concerned: their rejection of the Prophet (s.) now became even more vicious. Thus a group of his followers, including his son-in-law 'Uthman, already in 615 sought and found refuge and asylum for some time in Abyssinia.

Soon, in 622 CE, in order to survive the entire Muslim population left in Makkah had to emigrate to the oasis Yathrib, some 400 km to the north. This event–al-hijra–was of world historical importance and became the starting date for the Muslim calender. It being based not on the sun but on the moon, the year 2007 CE partially coincided with the year 1428 A.H. (anno Hijri).

Having arrived in Yathrib on Monday, 31 May, 622 CE, the oasis was renamed al-Madinah ("the City", scil. of the Prophet). Muhammad (s.) here created the first Islamic State as a federation of both Muslim and Jewish tribes whose relationship was governed by the first written constitution of the world, dictated by him. This State was indeed revolutionary and innovative by no longer linking citizenship to race, tribe or language but exclusively to religion (49: 13). Didn't verse 10 of Surat 49 (al-Hujurat) proclaim "All believers are brothers"?

As a result, al-Madinah became an ideological State, following a true change of paradigm. Its citizens became the germinating cell for what today is a world-wide community of brothers and sisters in Islam, affectionately known as "Ummah", a middle-of-the-road brotherhood and sisterhood (al-ummah al-wasatiyyah; 2: 143) that in fact without fail always managed to avoid fanaticism, imbalances, and extremes.

Being in a military situation of strategic defense, Muhammad (s.) with remarkable diplomatic skill, charismatic leadership and prowess on the battlefield tactically always seized the offensive in order to guarantee the survival of his embattled community, considered by Makkah as a mortal ideological threat. The military encounters between the two cities began with a skirmish at Badr, in 624, where 312 Muslim warriors individually and collectively defeated 950 fighters from Makka.

In retrospect, the war between Makka and al-Madinah (622-630) seems insignificant in terms of manpower, weaponry and casualties; yet its impact on world history could not have been greater. Altogether only 240 Muslims were killed on the battlefield during those years. They suffered their greatest losses–70 warriors–in 625 during the siege of al-Madinah, ending with the near disastrous battle at Mount Uhud.

At long last, in 628, Muhammad managed to stage a diplomatic coup by concluding, at Hudaybiyyah near Makkah, an armistice which anticipated the final surrender of the city in 630. When the Muslims occupied Makkah, they surprised everyone by proclaiming a general amnesty, foregoing revenge.

In 622, Muhammad (s.) the widower married 'A `isha, the young but extraordinarily intelligent daughter of Abu Bakr, his best friend and later his successor as first caliph. As head of State, the Prophet concluded 12 further marriages, mostly for dynastic reasons and therefore, in some cases, pro forma. Marriages at that time created family bonds which helped to create new alliances and to cement old ones. In fact, all of the later wives of the Prophet were divorcees or widows needing protection. All his wives carried the prestige of being "mothers of the believers" (umm al-mu`minin).

Soon after his "farewell pilgrimage" in 632, famous for his farewell speech at 'Arafat, Muhammad (s.) died in al-Madinah without leaving male heirs. He was buried where he had died, in 'A`isha`s room, which soon was made part of the Prophet`s Mosque. Today, this mosque–like the one in Makkah–can hold 800. 000 people for prayer.

MUHAMMAD AS A PERFECT BEING

As his biography makes clear, Muhammad (s.) was not the inventor of Islam but a deserving vessel for receiving and transmitting divine messages to mankind. Therefore, in spite of their high esteem for their Prophet, Muslims neither see him as the founder of their religion, nor as a supernatural being or as an incarnation of God. Consequently, Muslims object when they are called "Muhammadans" or when people speak of "Muhammadan Law" or "Mohamedism". In contrast to Jews ("Mosaic faith"), Christians, Buddhists and Zoroastrians, they want to be known not by a foundational figure but merely and abstractly as "Muslims", i.e. people "submitted to God".

Muhammad (s.) is the most maligned personality of world historical importance. This is a fact. But non-Muslims should be aware of how offensive any abuse of Muhammad is to Muslims, as proven by the infamous Rushdie affair.

For Muslims Muhammad (s.) was and is *al-insan al-kamil* (the perfect man) par excellence: pious, modest, ascetic, compassionate, reliable, peaceful, courageous, and wise–a model father, spouse, friend, profession-al, judge, soldier, diplomat, law-giver, statesman. In short, a person who succeeded in all he touched. Perfection, in Muslims' eyes, results from the optimization of all God given natural traits (al-fitra) of a human being: a mystic during the night and a soldier, defending his faith and his society, during the daytime.

This way, Muhammad (s.) may be valued for what he was in Confucian circles where the ideal of the unity of king and sage still is alive. But the Christian ideal of the perfect man is totally different. For them Jesus–a tragic man without professional career, family or children, and withdrawn from public life–became the prime model. It is not by mere chance that Christendom produced characters similar to Jesus, for instance in Don Quixote and Hamlet.

Also Islam has produced perfect "all-around" personalities in the image of Muhammad (s.), beginning with 'Umar ibn al-Khattab, the second caliph (634-644) and 'Ali ibn Abi Talib, the fourth one (656-

661). But also Salah ad-Din (d. 1193), the gentleman warrior who freed Jerusalem from the Crusaders, followed his prophet's mould. So did Ibn Taymiyyah (1263-1328), the great, militant Hanbali theologian who personally fought the Mongols. During the 19th century, both the Algerian freedom fighter, 'Abd al-Qadir al-Jaza'iri, and the Sudanese Mahdi made a name for themselves as insan al-kamil in Muhammad's footsteps.

THE ORIGINS OF THE QUR'AN

Every time the Prophet received a revelation–when a message "came down" (nazala) to him–he communicated it to the Muslim community, indicating where the new text was to be inserted into the body of the Qur'an as it then existed. Last not least by reciting the new revelation during public prayer, he made sure that hundreds of Muslims at any given time would know the Qur'anic text by heart. For this purpose, Muhammad (s.) used to recite the entire Qur'an once or twice during Ramadan.

Simultaneously he dictated new material to his chief secretary, Zayd b. Thabit who wrote it down on papyrus, flat stones and bones, pieces of leather, and palm leaves, keeping the whole orderly tied together. This was not an easy matter since revelations reached the Prophet over a period of 22 years. Thus the "Book" (al-kitab) during his lifetime was a loose-leaf collection (as-suhuf) that could only be completed after his death.

Accordingly Abu Bakr, the 1st caliph, immediately gave orders to Zayd b. Thabit to consolidate the text of the Qur'an as it stood at the Prophet's death. Zayd appealed to the public to come forward with any possible verse that might have escaped him. Then, in collaboration with the best Qur'anic experts in al-Madinah he finalized his collection.

After the death of Abu Bakr this first "copy" of the Qur'an was handed over to 'Umar, the 2nd caliph. When he, too, died his daughter Hafsa, a widow of Muhammad (s.) became guardian of the precious bundle.

Given the growing need of copies of the Qur'an for distribution throughout the expanding Muslim empire, and given the new availability of parchment, 'Uthman, the 3rd caliph, gave orders to Zayd b. Thabit to oversee the production of several identical copies on the basis of the collection preserved by Hafsa. This happened in 650/651 CE. 'Uthman then gave orders to destroy any existing private records of the Qur'an.

The handful of copies thus produced, except for 'Uthmans own copy, were sent to regional centers of Islam, like Kufa and Basra. Two of these first parchment copies still exist: 'Uthman`s copy is on display at the Topkapı Museum in Istanbul, the second one is preserved in Tashkent.

Equally important for safeguarding God`s message to Muhammad was the fact that tens of thousands of Muslims at any time (and as well today) committed the Qur'an to their memory. This alone made any possible attempt at forging the text a hopeless undertaking. Many Muslims always knew the Qur'an as they know their sons (6: 20).

In fact, there is a divine promise that the Qur'an will be preserved integrally to the end of days (15: 9).

When a decade ago thousands of snippets of Qur'anic verses were found in a mosque in Sanaa (Yemen), certain Western anthropologists believed that they had a case against the authenticity of the Qur'an. However, these snippets were not alternative versions but to more than 99 percent corresponded perfectly to the Qur'anic text as it stands.

The Yemeni snippets were private records that had not been destroyed as ordered by 'Uthman but rather, out of devotion, only "buried" (in sacks) in the mosque. The very few and only insignificantly deviating versions are due to the very large distance between al-Madinah and Sanaa. People there were not always able to catch up with the progress of revelation.

Western Orientalists had always known that. They are mostly convinced that the Qur'an as we know it today is identical with the text compiled in 651 CE. Indeed, aside from some self-serving Zionist attacks, most Orientalists consider the Qur'an as absolutely authentic. They appreciate that it is the first book ever written in Arabic and the best documented scripture of late antiquity.

Of course, today's Arabic script has considerably evolved with respect to its origins in the 7th century CE. At that time there existed no signs yet for punctuation, no question marks, no "diacritical" signs indicating, e.g., short vowels, duplication of letters, the absence of vowels (sukun) or aids for pronunciation like *hamza*. As a result, the earliest Qur'anic manuscripts served more as a memory aid for people who knew the text by heart and less as a determinant for pronunciation.

In fact, even though the Qur'an was revealed in the dialect of the Quraish, the dominant tribe of Makkah, the Prophet allowed every Arab to pronounce the Qur'an his usual way. This liberal procedure helped to bring out the wealth of meaning rather than causing semantic conflicts.

For example, to this day it is possible in the 4th verse of Surat al-Fatiha either to read "malik" (king) or "maalik" (ruler)–obviously without theological consequences.

THE AUTHORITY OF THE QUR'AN

Computer analysis clearly established linguistically that the Qur'an has only one single author. The same way it was established that the language profile of Muhammad (s.), gained from the vast collections of his sayings (ahadith), is quite different from the language profile of the Qur'an. In other words, it is scientifically proven that the Prophet did not invent the revelations he transmitted.

The same can be deduced from the fact that the Qur'an contains several passages heavily criticizing the Prophet's behavior. If he had been the author, would he have entered as embarrassing a text, critical of himself, as 80: 1-11?

Thus the only real question concerning Muhammad (s.) and the Qur'an is whether he truly was a prophet. This is of course a typical question for faith and of faith only, even though native Arabic speakers maintain that the Qur'an is a miracle (al-mujiza) for being inimitable linguistically (al-ijaz). Non-Arab speakers are more impressed by other features like the astonishing compatibility of the Qur'an with natural history, cosmology and any other modern scientific discovery. This is indeed remarkable, especially in contrast with the Bible. Nevertheless it would be a great mistake to see the Qur'an as a natural science textbook.

During the 9th century, Muslims split over the question whether the Qur'an was God's eternal word (umm al-kitab) and therefore "uncreated" (43: 4) or rather a historical event and therefore "created". For contemporary Muslims the Qur'an is both. In as much as God is outside of time and space, the Qur'an's origin is indeed timeless. But its entry into human history can be timed.

QUR'AN TRANSLATIONS

Only its original Arabic text deserves to be called "Qur'an" (recitation). Therefore Muslims like Muh. Ahmad Rassoul call their translations "The approximate meaning of the Qur'an into the German language", or similarly.

Conscious of the fact that every translation is an interpretation –and every interpretation a reduction–the Muslim world for a millennium resisted translations of their holy book. Thus with Hermannus Dalmata and Robertus Ketenensis in Toledo it was Christian interpreters who, in 1143, on the orders of Petrus Venerabilis, Abbot of Cluny, produced the first translation of the Qur'an into an Occidental language: Latin.

It was again due to a Christian initiative–by Martin Luther!–that this translation was printed in Basle, in 1543.

The oldest known Qur'anic translations into Latin by Englishmen are by Alexander Ross (London 1648) and George Sale (London 1734).

Today, we dispose of dozens of translations into English of which the most popular are by Marmaduke Pickthall (London 1930), Yusuf Ali (Lahore 1934-1937) and Muhammad Asad (Gibraltar 1980).

ISLAMIC THEOLOGY

F our of the Muslims` five "pillars of faith" are described in the Qur'an as follows:

...They all believe in God, and His angels, and His revelations, and His messengers, making no distinctions between any of them,... (2: 285; also see 4: 136 which mentions the fifth pillar: belief in the Last Day)

BELIEF IN GOD
God`s Most Beautiful Names

Muslims believe in the existence of a single, personal God, Creator and Preserver of the universe, both transcendent and immanent to it. Does the Qur'an not say:

We are closer to him [man] than his jugular [neck] vein (50: 16) but also:

No human vision can encompass Him whereas He encompasses all human vision (6: 103) and Never can you see Me! (7: 143).

What Muslims dare to say about God–whom they call "Allah" (as Arabic Christians do)–is absolutely limited to what God over time revealed about Himself. In the Qur'an can be found plenty of "God`s most beautiful names" (al-asma al-husna) which must all be understood as God`s attributes of perfection. Examples are al-wadud (Lover; Loved One) and al-muntaqim (Revenger).

These attributes obviously relate to each other in a dialectical manner and therefore seem to be contradictory while being compatible: this is the only way of at least vaguely indicating some of God`s majestic being. Surah 59: 22-24 offers the broadest list of divine properties:

He is Allah except whom there is no God, Knower of the invisible and the visible. He is the Beneficent, the Merciful. He is Allah except Whom there is no God: the Sovereign, the Holy, the Pacifier, the Giver of Faith, the Guardian, the Majestic, the Compeller, the Superb.

Remote is He from all they associate with Him. He is Allah, the Creator, the Formgiver, the Fashioner. His are the most beautiful names. All that is in the heavens and on earth glorifies Him. And He is the Mighty, the Wise (my translation).

There are sundry anonymous lists of God's most beautiful names, all registering exactly 99 such attributes as found in Qur'an and Sunnah. Beautifully calligraphed, one can find the most traditional of these catalogues in many Muslim homes as wall decorations.

God's secret 100th name is missing: a way of recalling that all human attempts to seize God's ultimate reality are futile.

Ar-Rahman and *ar-Rahim* are the very attributes of God most frequently mentioned in the Qur'an. This assures man that God, both in principle and action, is quintessentially compassionate and gracious; in fact, God is seen as having **prescribed for Himself mercy** (6: 12, 54). Indeed, except for the 9th Sura (dealing with warfare) all other Surahs open with the so-called basmala: **In the name of God, the Compassionate, the Merciful!** (*bismi'llahi-r-rahmani-r-rahim*). With this formula—or at least by saying "bismillah!" Muslims start any activity, whether they are about to drink a gulp of water or to insert the car key into its lock.

GNOSTIC TEMPTATIONS

The concept of God as illustrated by His "most beautiful names" is incompatible with monistic interpretations of reality, be it *materialistic* monism (Materialism; Positivism; Scientism) or *idealistic* monism (Platonism; Idealism; Gnosticism). Nevertheless a number of Muslim philosophers flirted with the neo-Platonic world vision of Plotinus (d. 270), the influential gnostic mystic. This was no less than a (failed) attempt of bringing about a change of paradigm: from the orthodox Qur'anic concept of God to a theosophical one.

This attempt had to fail because main-stream Muslims never overlooked that *intellectually* God can only be defined in negative terms in the sense of a *theologia negativa*: as the One Whose non-existence is unthinkable.

EVOLUTION OR CREATION ?

In the 20th century, many Muslims (like many fundamentalist "Creationist" Christians) thought they had to reject, lock, stock and barrel, all of Charles Darwin's research as well as the evolutionary conclusions drawn from it. This conflict has since subsided. Most people now realize that Darwin never was able to produce evidence for his thesis of human development through mutation. On the other hand, computer literate modern Muslims find no difficulty visualizing that creation may be a process based on a complex and cybernetic programming set into motion by God from time immemorial.

BELIEF IN HIS ANGELS

If one believes in the existence of a transcendental God it follows that there may be a non-perceptible, immaterial world–that reality does not end at the limits of our rather unreliable sensual perception. The Qur'an indeed teaches us that between heaven and earth, between God and mankind, there is a spiritual world, including angels like Gabriel (Jibril), Michael (Mikail), two Guardian Angels for each of us (13: 11), angels of death and chastisement (96. 18). We also learn about jinn, i.e. either helpful or mischievous spirits of lower rank (72: 11,14).

It has become a "cult" to deal with angels. Muslims, however, are aware that we cannot know more about the world of angels and jinn than what has been communicated to us *indirectly* in holy scriptures. Given our linguistic limitations we can be informed on that subject only metaphorically and allegorically.

It is therefore fruitless to debate whether Satan (al-shaytan) is a rebellious jinn or a "fallen" angel. It is much more important to explain that Satan having no power over man (14: 22) is not to be seen as a countervailing *opponent* of God, in the Manichean sense, but only as a seducer, a mere *instrument* in God's plan of salvation.

BELIEF IN HIS PROPHETS
True and False Prophets

Christians are expected to honor all Jewish prophets listed in the Old

Testament. In turn, Jewish people only accept these prophets, to the exclusion of Jesus.

In this respect Muslims are most generous. The Qur'an mentions 25 prophets–from Adam, Job, and Noah via David, Solomon and Moses to John the Baptist and Jesus. Thus Muslims recognize all biblical prophets (2: 136; 3: 84; 29: 46). In their view, human beings cannot reach any rank higher than prophethood.

THE SEAL OF PROPHETHOOD

From the Muslim perspective, the history of prophethood came to a close with Muhammad (s.) because through the divine revelation of the Qur'an, God, once and for all, restored the conceptually supreme Abrahamic faith in God, the One and Only.

In the Qur'an (33: 40) Muhammad (s.) has been designated the "seal of prophethood" (al-khatam). In addition, at 'Arafat, on the 9th day of the months of pilgrimage (dhul-l-hijja) in 632 the following was revealed:

Today have I perfected your religious law for you and completed My favor for you, and willed that Islam (self-surrender) be your religion (5: 3, sentence no. 5).

In fact, since then the world has never again seen another prophet, even though Baha'ists, Qadiani-Ahmadis and Mormons may see this differently. At any rate, people holding such a view cannot be considered Muslims.

The Christian churches treat certain sects–like Jehova's Witnesses and Mormons–as being outside their fold. In the same way Muslims view the Ahmadiyyah sect (both the Lahore and the Qadiani branches), Alevites (both the Turkish and the Syrian brands), Baha'ists, and Druses as well as certain extremist Shi'ites as being outside Islam. After all, every religious community has the right to define itself.

SINLESSNESS ?

According to Catholic and Orthodox dogmatics, at least, both Jesus and his "immaculate" mother Mary were free of sin. Similarly some

Muslims try to deduce from Qur'an and Sunnah that Muhammad (s.) was exempt from sin. They even speak of the cosmic pre-existence of Muhammad (s.), as a divine spark (nur Muhammadi), considering the Prophet as God's first creation.

Such intellectualizing theological speculations risk elevating Muhammad (s.) to a supernatural level, near divinization. These attempts conflict, however, with many Biblical narrations of grave misdeeds committed by prophets, like David, repeated in the Qur'an (38: 22 ff.). Muhammad would have been the first to protest any attempt at denying his purely human status. Indeed, on several occasions he was severely reprimanded in the Qur'an (80: 1-11; 9: 43; 17: 73-75; 18: 23 f.; 33: 37).

Muslims who in their majority shun pious exaggeration in any form rather distinguish between the inerrancy of the Prophet's teachings and his human fallibility in banal matters .

BELIEF IN HIS SCRIPTURES

Muslims must respect all revealed scriptures as being of divine origin. However, the Qur'an only refers to a small part of the Bible–mostly Torah, Psalms, and the New Testament (al-injil)–and makes clear that the current versions of the Bible in many respects are unreliable. How could one neglect the fact that Jews, Orthodox, Catholic, and Protestant Christians cannot even agree on which books constitute the Bible.

In the course of Islamic history remarkable (but unsuccessful) attempts were made to accord the status of revealed and therefore holy scriptures to certain non-Biblical material, including books from Buddhism, Hinduism (Vedanta) and Zoroastrianism.

In practice, and when in doubt, Muslims will always give the Qur'an preference. In particular, the historical-critical approach of Christian theologians to the New Testament confirmed the Muslims' worst suspicions about the utter unreliability of all its parts except the letters by St Paul (which, however, are unacceptable since he never met Jesus).

Against this background it figures that the Qur'an for Muslims is the highest and final scriptural authority, it being the book **containing all that you ought to bear in mind** (21: 10).

But nature as well is a manifestation of God–another "book" whose signs (al-ayat) must be deciphered and contemplated just as much as the verses (also called *al-ayat*) of the Qur'an. Today Muslims are conscious of the fact that they cannot understand the universe without the Qur'an, nor the Qur'an without sufficient knowledge of natural science. That is why religion and science never clashed during Muslim history. Both bodies of knowledge do not even overlap because religion alone deals with the ultimate causation of all being, with values, moral judgements, and with the qualitative aspects of life.

BELIEF IN LIFE AFTER DEATH
Beginning and End

"Nay, their knowledge of the life to come stops short of the truth", the Qur'an says in 27: 66. Thanks to their revelations, however, Christians and Muslims harbor similar eschatological images. Both take it for certain that the universe, created by God in time, will come to an end in time.

The narrations of genesis in Torah (at-tawra) and Qur'an differ, however, significantly. The Qur'an has science on its side in its assertion that the universe came into being as the result of the fission (Big Bang?) of extremely dense matter (21: 30), first appearing as gas formations (41: 11); that the universe is constantly expanding (51: 47); and that life arose in water (24: 45), the first living beings having been amphibious.

The Qur'an also drastically narrates the end of the universe as a cosmic catastrophe when the Hour has come, unexpectedly, and the trumpet will be blown, announcing the Last Day, the very day **"which shall turn the hair of children grey"** (72: 17).

HEREDITARY SIN?

According to the Qur'an, God did not condemn Adam and Eve

after their disobedience in paradise. Rather He forgave them (2: 37; 20: 122). Therefore Muslims reject the fatalistic idea that mankind ever since should have be burdened by a "hereditary (or original) sin". The Qur'an is indeed absolutely clear about the fact that people will only be judged on their own personal merits or faults; nobody is responsible for what someone else did or, in Qur'anic language, **carries anybody else`s burden** (6: 164; 2: 134; 10: 41).

In the Muslim view the doctrine of original sin is a fateful invention of St Augustine with extremely tragic consequences in the course of human history, characterized by the Christian quest for "salvation", culminating in the interpretation of Jesus as "Saviour on the Cross".

Sin and Forgiveness

This is not to say that Islam is ignorant of the category of "sin". On the contrary, like Christians Muslims distinguish between venial (sagha`ir) and capital (kaba`ir) sins (4: 31). And Muslims, like Christians, trust that God, the Beneficent and Merciful, will forgive sinners who are sincerely sorry for what they did (at-tauba), willing to make up for it, and determined not to relapse (4: 110). Muhammad (s.) reported that God in a non- Qur'anic revelation (hadith qudsi) said:

Oh Son of Adam, even if your offenses mounted up to the heavenly clouds, I shall forgive you if you ask My forgiveness.

One specific sin called *shirk* ("association") in Arabic, God will never forgive: to assume other gods beside Him. This is the case as well if other things *de facto* become more important in peoples` lives, as it happens when they become addicts, be it of drugs, work, lovers, or applause (4: 48, 116; 39: 65).

The Qur'an teaches us that the fate of man is sealed with his death.

No intercession for the deceased is possible except by God`s leave (2: 255).

Even though there is no Muslim equivalent to the Tibetan Book of the Dead, in Islam there exist many (unofficial) colorful descriptions of what happens between death and resurrection (al-barzakh). Since the dead are outside of space and time, they all, no matter when they died, may feel that the Last Judgement–where they receive the record of their deeds– happens *immediately* after death.

HEAVEN AND HELL

Like the Gospel (al-injil) the Qur'an promises man life after death–as a gracious gift of God, not as ontological necessity. In considerable detail the Qur'an describes the undescribable: How the faithful are rewarded with eternal bliss in paradise (al-jannah), and how the evil-doers are punished in hell (al-jahannam) where it is impossible to live and impossible to die (20: 74).

Some hasty conclusions were drawn from the description of almond-eyed, eternally pure female partners (al-zawaj), serving men only in paradise as their play-mates (al-hur). Such interpretations overlooked that both terms–al-hur and al-zawaj–in Arabic are without gender which means that they cover both genders. Therefore one can safely read all Qur'anic descriptions of paradise as relating to both men and women.

Humanistic circles continue discussing whether eternal damnation to hell was compatible with God`s Benevolence and Mercy. Could one understand "eternal" in the Qur'an as meaning "for an incalculable period", given that God is ready to forgive, except shirk, whatever and whom He wills (4: 48, 116)?

PREDESTINATION OR FREE WILL?

In the course of Islamic history deterministic schools of thought appeared, and reappeared, regularly which wanted to raise the belief in predetermination (al-qadar) to the level of dogma. A certain prevalence of fatalism among Muslims is the result. Protagonists of this trend can of course refer to hundreds of supportive Qur'anic verses. Allah there is depicted as the One Who guides whom He wills and leads astray whom He wills.

The deterministic school of thought also seems to have logic on its side: How could a human being enjoy free will in the presence of a God Who is Omniscient and Omnipotent—Who knows beforehand how I will act and Who could prevent it?

At the same time, the Qur'an contains hundreds of other verses that seem to support the idea of free will. One of them even acknowledges that man has accepted from God the responsibility for his actions (33: 72).

Therefore, Islamic history always knew as well schools of thought supportive of the notion of free will. Is Allah not impeccably Just, rewarding or punishing only according to merit and urging man to do what is right and to stay away from what is wrong? In particular 8: 53 is relevant in this context because Allah, in this verse, tell us that he will not change the situation of a people **until they first change their inner selves.**

This school of thought, too, seems to have logic on its side: How could Allah, the Merciful and Just, punish someone for doing what he could not help doing?

No wonder that all attempts by Muslim philosophers to reconcile the two theories of absolute predestination (al-jabr) and absolute free will failed. Muhammad (s.) had indeed warned Muslims against racking their brains over this insoluble issue. It is insoluble because it is linked to the very nature of God that is inaccessible to human reasoning.

Over time the two schools of thought neutralized each other. As a result, many Muslims in theory go by the notion of predetermination but in practice act as if they possessed free will. One has indeed the impression that Muslims apply predetermination more to the past than to the future.

While it is true that Muslim philosophers and theologians cannot cope with the issue under discussion they at least keep it alive. Muslims know that there is a problem. Occidental people, however, shove it under the rug, remaining oblivious of the entire problematics.

WORSHIPING IN ISLAM

The main obligations of a Muslim as worshiper are called the "Five Pillars of Islam" (al-arkan al-Islam). The Islamic community would indeed collapse if only one of these five pillars would rot. They are in fact mutually supportive. Together they form the moral fiber (al-akhlaq) of model Muslims. During pilgrimage, all five pillars are even bundled together.

CONFESSION OF FAITH

The two-part formula for the Islamic confession of faith (ash-shahada) reads as follows:

I give witness that there is no deity except Allah, and I give witness that Muhammad is Allah's messenger. In Arabic: Ashhadu an la ilaha illa`llah, wa ashhadu anna Muhammad ar-rasulu`llah.

Pronounced consciously and willingly in front of two witnesses, this formula formally turns a person into a Muslim.

Of course it takes more to transform someone confessing his belief (muslim) into somebody who fully interiorizes his faith to the point of becoming a true believer practicing Islam (mu`min).

The Arabic term "Islam" is derived from the linguistic root (masdar) s-l-m and can mean both "submission" (inferred from the verb *aslama*) or "peace" (inferred from the verb *salama*). Accordingly, a Muslim is someone who finds peace through submission to God, and Islam is the religion which brings this personal state about (3: 19).

Submission is a mental attitude characterized by nearly permanent consciousness of one's total dependency on God. It results in an almost constant desire to communicate with Him in a manner implying both exhortation and warning (adh-dhikr).

"Remembrance of God is indeed the greatest [good]" (29: 45). God-consciousness (at-taqwa; 48: 26) is indeed what distinguishes, and sets apart, a true Muslim; his piety enlivens his shahada.

Muslims are critical of the Western habit of separating things belonging together–their dualisms of Faith and Good Works (Luther), private and public morals (Machiavelli) or of matter and spirit (Descartes). Islam teaches Muslims to see reality holistically. Therefore, discussions as between Catholics and Protestants about "salvation through faith alone" or "through faith and good works" sound unreal to them. Muslims cannot conceive of a man who merely believes, without direct effect on his behavior. Surat al-Assr (103) takes this as given:

...Verily, man is in loss, except for those
who believe and do good works
and exhort one another to truth
and exhort one another to steadfastness.

PRAYER
Ritual Prayer

A Muslim can pray whenever and wherever he feels like it and in whatever language suits him best. However, in addition to such private prayer (du`a) he is obliged every day to offer five ritual prayers (as-salat; Farsi: namaz). These formalized prayers must be performed

- at specific times
- in a state of ritual purity (through washing hands, arms up to the elbows, face, ears, neck and feet (wudu; 5: 6)
- in Arabic
- facing the direction of Mecca (al-qibla)–without forgetting that **true piety does not consist in turning your faces towards the east or the west** (2: 177).

Ritual prayer can be performed alone, without an Imam leading it. It is, however, recommended that Muslims pray together.

The correct time for ritual prayer is determined by the positioning of the sun. Morning prayer (al-fajr) takes place shortly before sunrise, the second prayer (az-zuhr) in the early afternoon, the third (al-assr) in the late afternoon, the fourth (al-maghrib) shortly after sunset, and the last prayer (al-'isha) about 90 minutes later. This allows people to work without interruption during the most active part of the day, from sunrise until after the sun has passed its zenith. People travelling are allowed to shorten and to combine most of their prayers. Ritual prayer–whether prayed entirely aloud (like the morning prayer), partially aloud (like the afternoon and evening prayers) or silently (like the noon-time and afternoon prayers)–is structured around two different prayer units (ar-raka´at). All of these consist of regular recitations, invariably including the 1st Surat al-Fatiha. Some prayer units are to be complemented by additional Qur'an recitations whose choice is optional.

During the first prayer unit the Imam normally will recite a Qur'anic passage that is longer than the one chosen for the second raka´a, for instance the so-called Verse of the Throne (2: 255):

God–there is no deity save Him, the Ever-Living, the Eternal. Neither slumber overtakes Him nor sleep. His is all there is in the heavens and on earth. Who is there who could intercede with Him, save by His leave? He knows that which is before and which is behind them, whereas they cannot grasp any of His knowledge, save what He wills. His throne encompasses the heavens and the earth, and their preservation does not tire Him. And He is the Sublime, the Tremendous.

Morning prayer consists of two prayer units, the noon-time prayer, the afternoon prayer and the night prayer of four, and the evening prayer of three. Each prayer unit invariably begins with a recitation of the first, the "opening" Surat al-Fatiha, those "seven oft-repeated verses" (15: 87) whose importance in Islam can only be compared with the Lord`s Prayer (Paternoster) in Christendom:

In the name of God, the Gracious, the Merciful. Praise be to God, Lord of all the worlds, the Gracious, the Merciful, King on the Day of Judgement.

You alone we worship, and to You alone we turn for help. Guide us the straight way–the way of those whom You have blessed, not of those who have earned Your anger nor of those who go astray.

The Muslim way of praying involves mind and body. Muslims while praying are not sitting in a bench or kneeling occasionally. They stand, bow down, throw themselves onto the floor, sit on the floor (on their left foot), and keep bodily contact with their neighbors to the left and to the right. Their movements are synchronized, following those of the Imam who announces changes of position by calling out "Allahu akbar", literally "God is greater". (The real meaning of this command is of course that "God alone is great" since He is greater without any point of comparison.)

Given that praying means entering into dialogue with one's Creator and Sustainer, i.e. the most essential of all communications, a Muslim who fails to pray does not deserve this title. Surely, the level of his moral behavior will correspond to the quality of his prayer. A devout Muslim prays his "obligatory" prayers because out of his love for God he cannot live without. His prayers answer a meditative necessity of life.

Friday Prayer

Friday prayer–corresponding to the Christian Sunday worship–takes the place of the normal noon-time prayer and follows a sermon (al-khutba) delivered from a pulpit (al-minbar) by a preacher (al-khatib), normally identical with the regular Imam of the mosque. Most pulpits are modeled after the one maintained in the Prophet's Mosque in al-Madinah and are thus reached via stairs.

Traditionally, the preacher holds a stick, representative of his authority, and divides his sermon into a more theoretical and a more practical part, shortly sitting down in order to divide the two visibly as well. Outside the Arab world at least parts of the *khutba* are delivered in one of the local languages.

Normally, the *muadhdhin* calls twice for prayer (al-adhdhan). For the Friday service, however, his call is being sounded three times. First to call people to the mosque; secondly to announce the beginning of the sermon; and thirdly to announce the beginning of the ritual prayer, in this case only two *raka'at*. If at all possible, attending Friday prayer is a must for all male Muslims; women may participate if they so wish.

PRAYING IN ARABIC

Ritual prayer is performed in Arabic, entirely. It would, however, be wrong to conclude from this preference that Islam is an Arabic religion or a religion for Arabs only. The choice of Arabic rather is due to the Muslims' desire to use the very vernacular, in fact the very words, in which God in His Qur'anic revelation had addressed them. Therefore every Muslim tries to learn at least some basic Arabic, with a restricted vocabulary, hopefully better than Catholic altar-boys master their little Latin.

Thanks to the Muslims' high appreciation, Arabic is unique in being the only existing language that maintained its vitality during more than 1400 years, essentially remaining the same. Indeed, high Arabic (al-fusha) still is the *lingua franca* for Muslim theologians and intellectuals world-wide. In contrast, no Frenchman, British or German person today would understand someone speaking their languages the way they had been pronounced and composed 1000 years ago.

One can easily recognize Muslims because of their habit of integrating some Arabic into their speech, saying for instance *al-hamdu li`llah!* (God be praised), and–when astonished–*subhan`allah!* (God be glorified). Also frequently one hears *insha`allah* (God willing; 18 :23 f.) or–protectively–*ma sha`Allah* (may God keep it that way). Addressing each other, when meeting and when taking leave, Muslims say *as-salamu 'alaikum!* (peace be with you) to which the response is *wa 'alaikum as-salam!* (and with you, too, peace). In the course of conversation one is likely to hear as well *mabruk!* (congratulations), *barakatu`llahi fik!* (God bless you), *wa`llahi, bi`llahi!* (definitely), *jazak Allahu khairan!* (great thanks to God) and *ya Allah!* (my God!).

Non-Arabic Muslims could of course express the same in their mother tongues. On the other hand, introducing Arabic terms into other languages is an old tradition. In fact, when the Arabo-Islamic civilization globalized, from the 8th to the 14th centuries, as many Arabic terms penetrated European languages as American terms do today. It is quite telling that the Arabic vocabulary adopted at that time referred to luxuries or were taken from the fields of economics, technology, medicine, mathematics, and warfare, including–in this order–Coffee, Mocha, Sugar, Lemonade, Apricot, Rice, Syrup, Cinnamon, Ingwer, Muscat, Cumin, Jasmine, Lute, Drugs, Chess, Diwan, Sofa, Mattress, Lacquer, Benzine, Algebra, Algorithm, Cypher, Zero, Admiral, Arsenal, Cable, and Magazin–to name a few out of several hundred terms.

FASTING

Muslims do not only observe religious fasting (as-saum) during Ramadan. But only during that month do they fast continuously for 29 or 30 days. It is indeed obligatory for every Muslim health-wise capable to forego during this period eating, drinking, smoking, and sex from shortly before sunrise to sunset.

Ramadan is a lunar month. Therefore, like all Muslim calender events, from year to year it moves backwards by 11 days. Therefore, in high summer fasting may last no less than17 hours a day while in winter fasting is reduced to as little as 12 hours. Muslims living way up north–where the sun never sets in summer and never rises in winter–go by the fasting periods in the Muslim core countries.

It happens again and again that fasting does not commence every-where in the world on the same day. This is due to the fact that the new moon signalling the beginning of the month of Ramadan cannot be sighted everywhere *within the relevant time frame.*

Traditionally, what counts is actual visibility of the crescent, not its astronomically determinable appearance. Astronomical data so far are used for the *falsification* of a doubtful sighting of the moon but not yet generally for its *verification* , and this may cause considerable frustration. Should it not be possible that the entire Ummah accepts the moon as sighted in Mecca ?

To do it right, a Muslim should not change his working hours and habits during Ramadan. In that case, he will miss out on one of the three daily meals. He works while it is light and sleeps when it gets dark, rather than sleeping during the daytime fasting period and moving all three meals into the dark hours, thus simply shifting day and night.

Only when fasting is done right will it produce its physical, spiritual, moral, and social benefits: a beneficial distance to the daily whirlyburly money chase; introspection; self-control; compassion with the hungry poor; reduction of cholesterol and surplus weight.

What a social boon it is to celebrate the breaking of the fast (al-iftar) in a circle of like-minded friends! Another important social aspect of Ramadan fasting is the traditional giving of food or money (zakat al-fitr) to the poor and needy just before the Breaking the Fast-Festival ('id al-fitr).

Tough as fasting may have been, the feeling of being reborn is so strong that many Muslims, as they enjoy the end-of-Ramadan festivities, are already looking forward to the Ramadan to come.

PILGRIMAGE TO MECCA

Every grown-up Muslim, healthy enough for it and financially capable, is under the religious obligation to perform the great pilgrimage to Mecca (al-hajj) once during his lifetime. *Al-Hajj* can only be performed during the first 10 days of the month of pilgrimage (dhu-l-hijja), *al-Umrah*, the so-called little pilgrimage, any time of the year.

Pilgrimage is a complex phenomenon known to all religions. So it is in the case of *al-hajj*:

As far as *religious* history is concerned, the pilgrims in Mecca and surroundings virtually re-enact crucial events in the life of Abraham (s.), his Arabic concubine Hajjar, and their off-spring Ismail, Abraham's first son, whom he was ready to sacrifice in a test of his total obedience to God (37: 102).

Islamically al-hajj is the re-enactment, in all detail, of pilgrimage rites as performed by Muhammad (s.), including the waiting (wuquf) in the plain of 'Arafat. There, clad in shrouds as on the Day of Judgement, the pilgrims continue to cry out: *Labbayk, Allahuma, labbayk!* (Here we are at Your disposal, oh our God, here we are!).

In terms of the *sociology of religion* the Mecca pilgrimage is a grandiose, absolutely peaceful international gathering of millions of like-minded people from all corners of the world, united in a brother-and-sisterhood without parallel.

Individually the pilgrimage is an enormous mental and physical effort, also without parallel. Not every pilgrim can cope with the correct fulfillment in terms of time and place of all the required rites–in Mecca, 'Arafat, Muzdalifa, and Mina–and that among 2,5 million co-pilgrims and, in summer, with temperatures exceeding 50° celsius.

Al-hajj terminates with the Festival of Sacrifice ('id al-adha), lasting three days spent in Mina near Mecca. Now every pilgrim offers an animal sacrifice (al-qurban), usually a lamb, as Abraham had done 3500 years ago with a ram (37: 107). But the pilgrims know that **their flesh and their blood do not reach Allah but only their devotion** (22: 37).

For the host country, Saudi Arabia, the obligation of all Muslims to perform pilgrimage translates into a huge organizational and logistical challenge, expressed in the king's title of "Guardian of the two inviolable Places". The Prophet's Mosque in al-Madinah has been enlarged to hold 480.000 people praying, so has the Mosque in Mecca, now holding 640.000 people praying, both mosques being aesthetic marvels. Even so, the influx of pilgrims must be limited. Currently for 1000 Muslims of any given country only one visa is issued.

Not only the tribulations are big, so is the benefit of pilgrimage. Only as a *hajji*, the highest title one can earn, one feels like a real Muslim. Only now can one visualize what it means to bow into the direction of Mecca. Pilgrimage is a caesura, a new beginning, a reorientation of one's life to the point of reducing one's past to a period of *jahiliyya shahsiyya* (period of personal ignorance).

The experience of the universality of the Muslim community (ummah) remains unforgettable as well. The moment one leaves al-Madinah and Mecca one is likely to be homesick for them.

TAXATION

The fifth pillar of Islam–but ranking in religious importance with prayer–concerns the paying of a fixed annual property tax (al-zakah). Muslims assess themselves and pay this tax normally during Ramadan (2: 277; 73: 20).

Originally the minimum amount taxable were 85 grams of gold or 595 grams of silver. What counts in terms of capital is not the annual gain, i.e. growth, but mere possession. Therefore one`s property is taxable, and diminishes, even if there was no economic activity at all. Zakah is indeed an incentive for putting one`s capital to (productive) work.

Originally only cattle were taxed as a means of production. Today all such means and modalities of income are subject to *zakat*–taxation, however only with respect to gains made and with a regressive rate of taxation, beginning at 2,5 %.

Zakah is not to be seen as alms (as-sadaqa) but as a genuine, obligatory tax, mainly for social and communitarian purposes of which the Qur'an mentions seven: Supporting the poor and needy; freeing prisoners; alleviating over-burdened debtors; aiding travellers ("sons of the road"); remunerating the public administration (including defense) and working "in God`s cause", i.e. the promotion of Islam (9: 60).

This Qur'anic tax did not, and does not, prevent Muslim States from introducing additional taxes to fulfill the same purposes, and others as well.

In terms of religious theory it is of the utmost importance that the Qur'an elevated the paying of taxes to the leval of a prime religious obligation, right next to prayer and pilgrimage: A testimony to the societal commitment of Islam and the solidarity of Muslims vis-à-vis the community in which they live. All this not only as "civic duty" but as part of their worshiping of God (al-´ibada).

Muslims living in non-Muslim countries or in secularized Muslim ones must decide to *whom* to pay their *zakah*. Debatable, too, is the question whether the zakat-obligation is partially or fully fulfilled by paying income tax to Western governments. After all, with these taxes

Western governments are able to finance some of the activities mentioned in 9: 60 (administration; defense; social care).

None of these countries spends, however, any money for the promotion of Islam, a major purpose of the quoted verse. In view of this, many Muslims in the West transfer at least part of their *zakah* to Islamic organizations there, including those involved in charity work, like "Muslim Aid".

FESTIVALS

Islam only knows of two public holidays, the Breaking the Fast-Festival ('id al-fitr) at the end of Ramadan and the Festival of Sacrifice ('id al-adha) at the end of Pilgrimage. On both days the festive prayer is held early in the morning, without the usual call to prayer (al-adhdhan). In contrast to Friday prayer, the 'id-sermons do not precede ritual prayer but follow it.

In addition, particularly in countries with a Shi'i population, the 10th day of the month of Muharram is commemorated as "Ashura"–Day, the day on which Hussein bin 'Ali, grandson of the Prophet, was killed in 680 at Kerbala near Baghdad in 'Iraq.

In some Muslim countries the birthday of Prophet Muhammad (s.) (maulid an-nabawi) does now play a certain role as well, as in Egypt (under Fatimide influence) and in Turkey (under Christian influence). In Saudi Arabia this trend is strictly rejected as an illegitimate innovation risking the gradual deification of Muhammad (s.) after the model of Jesus (s.).

Even less acceptable are the Shamanistic celebrations of Spring by Turkish and Kurdish Bektashi-Alevis, on 22 March, corresponding to the pre-Islamic Iranian New Year`s Day (Nowruz).

BURIAL

Burial is no "pillar" of Islam but nevertheless a part of worshiping. The ceremonies involved are conducted as follows:
• The corpse of the deceased is washed by members of the family, or under their supervision, wrapped in white linen

sheets and buried the day following his/her death, at the latest.

- The casket is put on the bier in front of his / her mosque. There, following the noon or afternoon prayer, the burial prayer will be spoken, while standing.
- Male relatives and or friends alternate in carrying the coffin to the hearse and follow it to the burial grounds; women are excused but not excluded from this duty.
- The corpse, taken from the casket, is put into the grave in such an oblique way that the eyes of the deceased are directed towards Mecca. (This way, all graves are parallel to each other and in a 90° angle towards Mecca.) In his sermon the Imam may remind the dead person of what to answer when asked by the angel of death: What his religion is, who his prophet is, and which is his book ?
- The relatives immediately fill in the grave with earth, plant flowers, and water them before leaving the grave. To erect monuments to the dead is, however, gravely disapproved of as an un-Islamic cult. Consequently, in Arab countries graves look pretty much neglected.

Muslims are not supposed to indulge in sorrow nor to mourn for more than three days. After all, God`s will was done, and hopefully the deceased now is with God. For Muslims, professional female mourners are particularly odious. Only widows are expected to observe a mourning period of no more than four months and 10 days. This rule is in consonance with the interdiction for widows to re-marry within three months of their husband`s burial, so as to discover whether they are pregnant or not before entering a new relationship (2: 228).

In some parts of Turkey as well as in Cairo people commemorate the deceased in his former home with Qur'an recitations and prayers, on the day of burial as well as seven days and 40 days later (mevlut).

This is, however, more of a Pharaonic and Christian than Islamic custom. Occidental law does not allow such speedy burials, if only not to lose eventual proofs of a major crime. Of course refrigeration there allows the storage of corpses for long periods.

Also, most Western legal systems forbid burials without coffins even though this delays the decomposition of corpses (and thus re-using of graves) considerably.

And only few cemeteries in the West possess sections where Muslims can be buried, correctly aligned versus Mecca.

In view of all this many immigrant Muslims in the Occident will continue to send their dead back for burial at home.

LAW AND ETHICS

LEGAL SOURCES

I slamic manners, etiquette, moral rules and ethics all have a legal basis. Islamic law in turn has the following foundations:

- the divine norms contained in the Qur'an (ash-shari'ah)
- the derived legal principles of the Qur'an (al-maqasid)
- the model behavior and teachings of the Prophet (his Sunna)
- the jurisprudence (al-fiqh) built by Muslim jurists from these bases through analogy (al-qiyas)
- and taking into account their consensus (al-ijma).

The latter "source" of law—rather a method of finding it—refers to the saying of the Prophet (s.): "My community will never agree on an error."

QUR'ANIC NORMS

Without any doubt, the Qur'an is primarily a theological text with moral guidance and not a legal code. It contains, however, about 200 verses normative in nature (out of more than 6200 verses altogether). These, in much detail, mainly deal with matters of family and inheritance. Yet there are also some legal rules of civil and criminal procedure, including the law of evidence. Finally there are a mere handful of norms concerning State, economics and penal law.

All of these, but only these, few Qur'anic norms plus the clear and unambiguous normative rules of the authentic Sunna as direct and eternal divine guidance (shar'Allah) deserve the name of shari'ah (literally " road to the watering place"). Thus it is misleading to reduce the meaning of shari'ah to criminal law.

PRINCIPLES OF THE QUR'AN

Of major importance for the development of Islamic jurisprudence are the general legal principles of the Qur'an (al-maqasid) which can be obtained through an analysis of its rationale and fundamental values. This provides pillars of a moral order based on justice, essential equality of all human beings, giving the common good preference over private interests, responsibility, promotion of the family as well as high estimation for kindness, honesty, reliability, incorruptibility, sincerity, cleanliness, bravery, compassion, generosity, patience, modesty, and similar virtues describing a model Muslim.

These principles play a decisive role whenever Islamic norms are to be interpreted or newly to be developed against the background of newly emerging issues.

THE SUNNA OF THE PROPHET

"Sunna" is a pre-Islamic term denoting model behavior (uswa hasana). This term also appears in the Qur'an in connection with God`s (unchangeable) way or habit (sunnat Allah, 33: 62). Nowadays, the concept "Sunna" is used in two different contexts: Either for the *normative* model behavior of the Prophet (33: 21) or for actions which are *recommended* without being obligatory, like voluntary, additional "*sunna* prayers". Frequently *sunna* is also used in the sense of "customary", for instance in opposition to improper innovations (al-bida', sing.) .

In the Qur'an we read again and again **And obey Allah and His messenger** (8: 46). And he was moved to say: **If you love Allah, follow me, and Allah will love you...!** (3: 31). This is the basis for accepting the recorded traditions of the Prophet as a second written source of the Islamic moral and legal code.

The traditions are of course recorded in so-called *hadith* collections of which six are canonical. They contain much of what the Prophet (s.) said (sunna qawliyya), did (sunna fi'liyya), or tolerated (sunna taqririyya).

Today *Hadith* and *Sunna* have become synonymous even though the former term is more associated with reports and the latter more with attitudes.

Many thousands of *ahadith* (pl. of hadith) have been collected, sifted, and systematized as from the fourth post-prophetic generation.

Among these voluminous hadith–collections the ones by al-Bukhari (d. 870), Muslim (d. 875), Ibn Maja (d. 892), Abu Dawud (d. 888), al-Tirmidhi (d. 892), and al-Nasa`i (d. 915) enjoy the highest prestige. They are called "the six authentic ones" (as-sahih as-sitta). Their prestige does not amount to a *proof* of correctness but to such an assumption .

When dealing with the Sunna one must keep the following considerations in mind:

(1) Nobody can become a proper Muslim on the basis of the Qur'an alone because many essential components of the teachings of Islam, including its moral code and rituals, are mainly if not entirely based on the Sunna. In some cases the Sunna is even indispensible for a proper understanding of the Qur'anic text itself. It makes eminent sense therefore to call the large majority of orthodox Muslims "Sunni Muslims" or Sunnites.

(2) The Sunna, inspired (not revealed) by God (al-wahy khafi) is an essential but secondary source of Islam. In other words: The Sunna has the sole function of explaining and complementing the Qur'an, but never to derogate it. Should there be a contradiction between the two, the Qur'an would always supersede the Sunna, never the reverse. In case of such a conflict one would have to assume that the hadith in question had been fabricated or misunderstood. (Alas, not all Muslim legal experts are agreed on that.)

(3) With a few exceptions called "holy hadith reports" (al-ahadith al-qudsiyya) the Sunna does not contain divine verbal revelations. Its authority rests on the fact that Muhammad in his person virtually embodied the Qur'an and on the already quoted divine command to follow the Prophet (s.) in matters of faith and morals, not in secular matters such as medicine, agriculture or warfare.

(4) The Prophet (s.) for some time had counseled against fixing the Sunna in writing in order to forestall any confusion between Qur'an and

Sunna. (For that very reason, in Qur'anic schools the Qur'an is taught exclusively, and no part of the Sunna.) As a result there are very few written hadith-reports contemporary with the Prophet (s.), like the lost one by 'Abdallah b. Amr b. As. On the whole, the Sunna was recorded some time after the death of the Prophet (s.) and can therefore not compete with the superb authenticity of the Qur'an.

(5) In the process of collecting, sifting, and preserving the hadith reports great care was taken to weed out possible forgeries. In particular the chain of traditionists (al-isnad) was scrutinized: Could they really have met? Does the chain end with a companion of the Prophet? Had any of the transmitters ever shown moral weakness? Could their memories still have been intact?

For the purpose of checking out these questions a biographical science was developed, with data on all the personalities appearing in any of the transmitter chains (with up to nine links). As historical scientists the famous hadith collectors by far surpassed any historiographic level of excellence obtained until then.

Nevertheless their material is not beyond any doubt whatsoever:

(a) In the original Islamic community of al-Madinah the concept of "Prophetic Sunna" was still unknown. Rather, law was administered on the basis of Qur'an and local custom (al-'urf) in as much as it did not contradict the revelation. This situation is clearly reflected in the "living Sunna" as recorded by Malik b. Anas in al-Madinah under the title al-Muwatta. At that time, people still spoke of the Sunna of Caliph Abu Bakr or the Sunna of Caliph 'Umar.

Only after Imam al-Shafi'i, a legal genius, had been successful in restricting the concept of Sunna to the traditions of the Prophet alone, it became tempting retroactively to attribute to him sayings which suited certain theological circles or ethnic groups.

(b) The great collectors of ahadith listed above while scrutinizing the chain of transmitters (al-isnad) shied away from doing the same to the transmitted material itself (al-matn) except in cases where the content of a hadith obviously was impossible or false. They did not feel entitled to play judge about anything the Prophet might have said or done.

Of course they did not have modern means of linguistic analysis and historical criticism. Therefore, their collections contain a number of reports which suggest some pious forgery at work and also reports which suspiciously favor a particular political or theological trend or certain tribes–issues that had not been critical at the time of the Prophet (s.)

Occidental orientalists like Ignaz Goldziher and Josef Schacht therefore felt justified to reject the entire Sunna, lock, stock and barrel. In doing so they failed to appreciate the oral culture of 7th century Arabia.

At that time, people performed near incredible feats of memorization, still equalled by contemporary "Hafidhs" who, already at the age of 10, succeed in committing the entire Qur'an to memory.

The mentioned orientalists overlooked as well that there were so many witnesses to the Prophet's behavior and sayings that the possibility of successful inventions was ruled out by social control. Finally, orientalists underestimated the religious awe of the early Muslims that would have prevented them from committing the atrocity of fabricating a lie against Allah or their Prophet.

This is not to say that certain traditions should not be challenged today. But that takes more knowledge than any of the Western orientalists ever possessed, except perhaps for Harald Motzki. In his study of *The Origins of Islamic Jurisprudence–Meccan Fiqh before the Classical Schools* (Brill, 2002) he comes to the considered conclusion that the early Islamic sources are highly reliable.

For the reality of Islam in our time it is even irrelevant whether Western Islamologues are happy with the traditions of the Sunna or not. Because for 1400 years now this Sunna has thoroughly coined and colored and stamped Muslims. It penetrated into poetry (like al-Busiri's al-Burda), folklore, and proverbial wisdom, and it formed many habits of family life, child education, and even cuisine. After all, even a non-authentic Prophetic saying can be beneficial, like the popular "Seek knowledge even if (in as far away as) China".

ISLAMIC JURISPRUDENCE

Muslim jurists (al-fuqaha; s. al-faqih) proceed from the assumption that there is one single source of law only: God. Therefore, their main activity is not to prepare legislation but to find the law in Qur'an and Sunna. Only if no directly applicable norms can be found in either body of texts, legal experts are allowed to develop rules themselves. But that, too, on the basis of the legal principles of Qur'an and Sunna (al-maqasid). This is achieved by seeking analogies, keeping in mind the following criteria:
- the commonweal (al-maslaha; al-istislah)
- dire necessity (ad-darura)
- established custom (al-'urf)
- individual need (al-haja)
- continuity (al-istishab)
- preference (al-istihsan)

It does not take much imagination to see that this methodology permits Islamic jurisprudence to remain dynamic, flexible and problem-oriented, provided that the fuqaha keep in sight all possible implications, show enough courage and creativity, and preserve their sense of what is essential.

Even if modern laws are codified—whether they deal with the rules of street traffic, stock exchange control or gene technology—all such "secular" norms somehow must be anchored in Qur'an and Sunna.

In that sense all the laws and ordinances in a Muslim State are "Islamic" and valid only if in accordance with the divine *shari'ah*.

Thanks to this methodology Muslim lawyers over the centuries developed a magnificent, highly complex and sophisticated legal system, in terms of conceptuality and intellectuality second to none.

This Islamic body of law lays claim to universal validity. In fact, conceptually the Islamic legal system is historically the first one to qualify as *international* law (al-ahkam duwaliyya).

It is important to note that this development was autonomous, i.e. independent of the developments in the "neighboring" Roman law area. In particular the simultaneous existence of competing, private legal schools (al-madhahib) was a truly singular specificity of Islamic law. Even today seven major such schools exist. They tolerate each other even though they continue to be in disagreement on important points of law. All of these schools were founded by towering legal minds called "Imam":

- Abd Allah b. 'Ibad (7th cent.) ----> 'Ibadites
- Zaid b. 'Ali (d. 740), author of the oldest existent
  legal text book ----> Zaidites
- Jafar as-Sadiq (d. 765) ----> Twelver Shi'is
- Abu Hanifa (d. 767) ----> Hanafites
- Malik b. Anas (d. 796) ----> Malikites
- Muhammad Idris as-Shafi'i (d. 820), founder of Islamic
  jurisprudence as a legal science ----> Shafi'tes
- Ahmad b. Hanbal (d. 855) ----> Hanbalites (Wahhabi).

The Zahirite School of Law, best represented   by Ibn Hazm in Andalusia   (d. 1064) did not survive, probably because of its theoretical radicalism; as extreme literalists they had refused any interpretation of the Qur'anic text.

Even today, North Africa remains Maliki, Southeast Asia Shafi'i, Turkey Hanafi, Saudi Arabia Hanbali, the Iran Jafari , and the Yemen Zaidi. However, the practical importance of school differences is declining. Nowadays privately developed Islamic law in the classical sense is applied directly only in Saudi Arabia.

Muslims living in the Occident are enjoined by Islamic law to respect the local norms, as long as they can practice the Five Pillars of their faith, i.e. its essence.

In accordance with Qur'an and Sunna, Muslim States all through history had accorded Christian and Jewish religious minorities the right to practice most of their own laws (concerning ritual, family, inheritance, diet, and even criminal law) autonomously. Western countries, imposing their territorial sovereignty without any exception, are not as liberal. Therefore, Muslims in the Occident can abide by their religious norms—including family and inheritance law as well as the prohibition of interest on capital—only to the extent made possible through contractual arrangements and by making wills.

MORAL CATEGORIES

Islamic Jurisprudence which, as will be remembered, also covers matters of morality and etiquette, knows of absolutely obligatory (wajib) and absolutely forbidden (haram) actions. For instance, there can be no dispensation from prayer and no license to kill.

In between Muslim lawyers distinguish between actions which are recommended, i.e. desirable (mandub), and those to be avoided, i.e. undesirable (makruh).

Between these poles one moves on a large, morally neutral (mubah) territory. In fact, this neutral ground should be the largest since Islam follows the principle that everything not specifically forbidden is allowed. The Qur'an evens warns against ill-guided attempts to reduce man`s freedom of action under the pretext of piety: **Do not ask about matters which, if they were to be manifest to you, might cause you hardship** (5: 101). **After all, Islam wants to facilitate life, not complicate it** (2: 185; 22: 78).

Even so, a conscientious person will stay clear of things "merely" considered undesirable. Also, he / she will normally do what is "merely" recommended. As a result, in Muslim communities of Puritanical temper most things end up being either entirely black or entirely white, commanded or forbidden.

ALLOWED / DISALLOWED

It is impossible to list everything that Islamic ethics (al-akhlaq) allows, recommends or even orders to be done. It is more significant to focus on the Qur'anic rule that the moral quality of human behavior solely depends on his/her intentions (an-niyya). At any rate, Islamic ethics run parallel to the moral aspirations of all major civilizations. Thank

God it is no Islamic distinguishing characteristic that the life, bodies, honor, and property of others must be respected; that people should be just, kind, honest, truthful, clean, discrete, reliable and diligent.

Muslim theologians did not develop a list of Ten Commandments even though a Qur'anic passage would have warranted such an endeavor (6: 151 f.).

For a more detailed introduction to Islamic ethics the following should suffice:

- Suicide (al-intihar) is forbidden, without any qualification (4: 29). This also applies to suicide in stages, as in the case of smokers and alcoholics.
- All drugs which impair clear thinking or self-control are forbidden (5: 90). This command of soberness relates to natural or synthetic drugs even in the smallest quantity.
- To consume pork, blood products (black pudding), and meat from animals not slaughtered is forbidden (2: 173; 5: 3; 6: 145; 16: 115). In his book on "Animals in Islam" (1989) Al-Hafiz as-Masri lists 78 diseases related to the consumption of pork.
- The meat of vegetarian animals is allowed, provided they are halal for having been slaughtered ritually, i.e. the way kosher meat is produced. Muslims may, however, eat non-halal meat when invited to the table in a Christian home (5: 5).
- Fortune telling in any form, including astrology and reading from coffee grounds (al-fal), is forbidden.
- In contrast to guardianship (al-kafala) the legal adoption of children is not permitted.
- Men and women must dress in a sexually non-provocative manner. In the case of women this implies that in public only their faces, hands and feet ought to be visible (24: 31; 33: 59).
- While sexually arousing, rhythmically hypnotizing music

is condemned, morally elating "classical" music, both Arabic and Western is recognized as valuable. Moving Qur'an recitations (tartil; tajwid) and highly aesthetic calls to prayer (al-adhdhan) are sounds –not music– of a spiritual nature, like melodious Sufi contemplation (as-sama).

- Mixed social dancing, disco or classical style, is disapproved of.
- Tattooing, piercing, and beauty surgery (except in case of disfigurations) are disapproved of as violating the integrity of the human body.
* As extravagant luxuries the use of gold and silver table ware is not approved of. Men are not supposed to wear gold jewelry or silk clothes.
- Muslim men are supposed to wear a beard. Their mustache must not touch or even cover the upper lip.
- Circumcision of male babies is "sunna", originally based on a Biblical command (Genesis 17, 10).
- Female circumcision has no basis in Islam; rather it is forbidden for being mutilation.
- Muslims, men and women, should remove their pubic hair every 40 days.
- Muslims only eat with their clean hand, right-handers with their right, left-handers with their left hand, the other hand being used for cleaning purposes.
- Cloning of humans and systematic interference for the improvement of their genetic make-up is outlawed (4: 119). However, for the purpose of fighting diseases and disfigurations gene manipulation may be legal.
- Organ transplantation is acceptable. Muslims see brain death as the decisive moment ending human life.

HUMAN RIGHTS

The term "human rights" does not appear in any single sacred script. This is not surprising because from a religious standpoint individuals are seen as created by, and entirely dependent on, God. Whatever rights they have have been conferred on them by their Creator. Consequently, the very idea of rights rooted in man could only be conceived in the atmosphere of the American and French revolutions. It was only then, in the 18th century, that the first human rights declarations were promulgated.

It is nevertheless easy to prove that all the classical human rights as formulated in international covenants had already been guaranteed by the Qur'an 1400 years ago. This is true of both Human Rights Covenants of the United Nations and the one by the European Council.

Technically, the Qur'an safeguards human rights by way of reflexive claims: The general prohibition to kill can be read as giving everybody a right to live. The same is true for deriving a right to property from the prohibition of theft, and of the right of political participation from the command of consultation.

Since the Qur'an had already foreseen, and paved the way for, the abolition of slavery, in the context of human rights only two fields of conflict are left:

- The Qur'an allows corporal and, for a few major crimes, also capital punishment (5: 33, 38, 45; 24: 2).
- Islamic family law proceeds from the assumption that husband and wife in certain limited, gender-related respects are not alike; it therefore allows a role-specific differentiation.

Thus, on the whole, in the field of human rights the Islamic legal order is complementary and not antagonistic to the Western one.

LAW VERSUS MYSTICISM

Islamic law does not interfere as much, and in as great detail, in daily life as Mosaic (Talmudic) law does for orthodox Jews. Nevertheless, also Islamic law presents the danger that religion becomes too normative an affair, losing some of its spirituality in the process. Since a Muslim theologian cannot help simultaneously being a jurist, the danger of a Talmudization of Islam is not negligible.

In fact, all through Muslim history there have been two major reactive trends against the prominence of law in Islam–folk Islam and Islamic mysticism (Sufism).

FOLK ISLAM

"Folk Islam" designates the practice of this religion as encountered by simple people, close to nature, who find it difficult to cope with the totally abstract Islamic concept of God and the absence in Islam of intercession in favor of man by useful spirits and saints. The average Muslim may indeed feel a craving for touching something sacred, as Christians do with their baby Jesus in the manger.

Such psychological needs led of course to the development of heterodox forms of Islam and, depending on the area, its mixing with Shamanistic, Hinduistic, Christian, and pre-Islamic Arabic notions and superstitions. This explains why acts forbidden by Islam are widely practiced, like the adoration of living and dead saints (walis, pirs, and marabouts), black magic, fortune telling, drug-induced ecstacy dancing, and belief in miracles by human individuals used to invoke the protection of Jinns (72: 6).

Some orientalists like Annemarie Schimmel collected a maze of information on each of these deviations, under the title of "Phenomenology of Islam"; they remained un-Islamic, nevertheless.

Part of folk Islam is an excessive veneration of the family of the Prophet (s.), supposedly justified by 33: 33. His descendants are called Sharif if their family tree goes back via Muhammad`s grandson Hassan. Those tracing their blood relationship with the Prophet back via his grandson Hussein are given the honorary title of Sayyid. Even now, 40 generations later and regardless of their moral behavior, they are being attributed a blessing power (al-baraka), conferred by touching them.

It would be more in conformity with the Qur'an to ask God`s blessing for Muhammad (s.) and his house (42: 23) and to honor his descendants in that way.

MYSTICISM

Sufism developed inside the Muslim world, as a genuinely Islamic movement, as a form of asceticism and intense piety that gave the love of God preference over the fear of Him. Sufism did a lot for the interiorization, i.e. the spiritualization, of Islam.

In this sense, Muhammad–who spent whole nights in prayer–was a Sufi, as were Hassan al-Basri, Rabi´a al-Adawiyya and other early Muslims. These already were **longing for their Sustainer`s countenance** (al-wahy; 13: 22, 92: 20). This attempt literally to "face" God, so typical of Sufis ever since, did not aim at any emancipation from His legal norms, the shari´ah. On the contrary, law abidance was at the foundation of their faith.

The Qur'an supports mystically tuned piety in several verses. The Light Verse (ayat an-nur; 24: 35) compares God with the fundamental phenomenon of light, allowing sight, color, and vegetal growth. Light–partially visible, partially invisible–is a physical constant, both as unsurpassable speed (the "speed of light") and as the smallest possible package of energy (Max Planck`s "quantum") which gave New Physics its name (Quantum Physics).

The Light Verse reads as follows:

God is the Light of the heavens and the earth.
The parable of His light is that of a niche containing a lamp.
The lamp is in a glass. The glass is like a shining star–
lit from a blessed tree, an olive tree neither of the east
nor of the west, whose oil would almost glow even though no fire
had touched it. Light upon light !
God guides to His light whom He wills.
And God speaks to men in parables,
for God (alone) has full knowledge of all things.

In contrast to early Muslim mysticism, a later phase–mainly from the 11th to the 15th century–saw a more intellectual and philosophical type of Sufi, strongly influenced by neo-Platonic and Gnostic views. Now the unio mystica of Christian mystics–becoming one with God–became the Sufis` highest aspiration.

At the same time, Sufis began to systematize the "Path" (to perfection), both through their publications and the creation of Sufi orders (at-turuq; s. at-tariqa) whose Shaykhs demanded from their followers the kind of absolute obedience frowned upon by the Qur'an (9: 31).

The Sufi orders differed mainly in terms of dress and the forms of their meditative sessions. Some practiced silent meditation, others accelerate their shouting to the point of ecstacy. Some used music, others rhythmical movements resembling dancing.

Some of these movements, in particular the Qadiriyya order of 'Abd al-Qadir Jilani of Baghdad (d. 1166), the more sober, central-Asian Nakshbandiyya order and the Mevlevi (Dancing Dervishes) inspired by Jalal ad-Din Rumi (d. 1273) not only survived but even thrive now in the Occident as well, now even accepting women and non-Muslims.

In fact, the Muslim world at any time during the last 800 years saw new Sufi circles and organizations appear on the mystic path. Two of them, Ahmad Tijani's (d. 1830) Tijaniiya and Ahmad al-Alawi's (d. 1934) Ahmadiyya, both created in Algeria, found resonance from Black Africa to Britain and the United States.

Best known among Muslims and non-Muslims are two Persian Sufis who were executed for heresy and blasphemy: Hussain Mansur al-Hallaj (d. 922) who had begun to feel one with God (: "ana al-haqq"/ "I am the truth") and Shihab ad-Din Suhrawardi (d. 1191), founder of a speculative mysticism of light.

Undisputedly the "greatest of all masters" (shaykh al-akbar) among Sufis was the Andalusian Muhy ad-Din Ibn 'Arabi (d. 1240 in Damascus). To this day Muslims debate his esoteric interpretation (ta'wil) of the Qur'an bordering, or crossing into, pantheism.

Like many other Sufis, Ibn 'Arabi has been accused of elitist arrogance and metaphysical speculation without limit, leading to his reinterpretation of the mainstream understanding of the Qur'an in a neo-Platonic/Gnostic manner. Typical in this vein are Sufi pronouncements like the one by al-Simnani (d. 1336) "I am the one whom I love, and the one whom I love am I."

At the core of Ibn 'Arabi`s teaching is the notion of *al-wahdat al-wujud*, the unity of all being. From this viewpoint, everything –all ideas as well as things–emanates from God, is His manifestation.

The world as we experience it, as a separate entity, is an illusion. Ibn 'Arabi claimed that the orthodox dualism (al-thanawiyya)–distinguishing between the Creator and his creation–violated the prime Islamic doctrine of the Oneness of God (at-tawhid).

Traditional Muslims see other dangers in Ibn 'Arabi`s thesis: Without God being different from me, how can I pray? Does the doctrine of *al-wahdat al-wujud* not lead straight into irresponsibility and immorality ?

The Indian Muslim Ahmad al-Sirhindi (d.1624), "2nd Millennium Renewer of Islam", countered Ibn 'Arabi`s doctrine with the thesis of *al-wahdat ash-shuhud* (unity of perception). He admitted that Sufis *experienced* all being as one. But he denied any *ontological* reality to their vision. From his point of view there is no dualistic danger as long as Muslims do not forget that the Being of God is categorically different from the derived existence of man. God is existence (wujud asli). His creation is not an illusion but totally dependent on Him in its existence to the point of only being a shadow of His (wujud zilli).

In accordance with this doctrine orthodox Muslims to this day do not maintain that God is *everything* but that everything is *from* God.

They deduct from the Qur'an that God is both immanent and transcendent.

Today`s Muslim world is shaped by a strong Puritan trend. Many Muslims are out to rediscover the pristine teachings of primitive Islam as lived in al-Madinah during the Prophet`s time. Both trends merge in the Salafi doctrine of Saudi Arabian and the Islamic Movement world-wide. Both reject Sufism (as irrational and untraditional) and metaphysical (Mu`tazili) Rationalism alike, treating both trends as inadmissible innovations in the area of faith (al-aqida).

THE MUSLIM FAMILY

Man and woman are equally addressed in the Qur'an as being of identical value before God, their Creator (33: 35). On earth their calling is the same: Submission to their God, i.e. Islam, so as to arrive at a blissful state in the hereafter, here and there as partners of each other (2: 25). Since man and woman complement each other, celibacy ("monasticism") is not considered in Islam as desirable. He/she who is capable of it should marry. This would normally happen on the basis of a marriage contract ('aqd an-nikah) in which, e.g., the financial contribution to his wife of the husband (al-mahr) is fixed, serving as security in case of divorce and an advance old age pension for her.

Man and woman, husband and wife, have the same religious rights and duties. Both pray, fast, go on pilgrimage, and pay zakat-taxes in equal manner. In marriage, both continue to dispose of their own property, alone. (No mixing of funds.) Both keep their pre-marriage names given at birth and the right to expand their professional and other abilities.

As everywhere, Islam, too, considers healthy families as the very foundation of all social units, extended family, tribe, nation. And like other religions Islam reserves the legitimate exercise of sexuality to the family, defending the family against any erosion, extra marital affairs, gay "marriages" or sexual perversities.

While preaching compassion for, and clemency for, people in sexual distress, Islam does not condone the propagation of homosexuality and lesbianism as legitimate life style "options" (7: 80 f., 11: 78 f.).

Ideally Muslim society is based on monogamous marriage, entered into by the free choice of both partners. In contrast to Christian weddings, marriage is not considered in Islam as a sacrament or as sacred. More sober (and realistic), Muslims regard marriage as a contract that, if need be, can be dissolved. Polygamy, limited to four spouses, is permitted under conditions which can be fulfilled only during extreme situations in which individuals or society as such find themselves (4: 3, 129).

Male Muslims can only marry women who believe in God, be they Jewish or Christian (5: 5). On the other hand, Muslim women are expected to marry Muslim husbands only. (This is concluded in analogy to 60: 10 and 2: 221.) However, a couple is only entitled to inherit from each other mutually if both partners are Muslim.

Within marriage Qur'an and Sunna provide for different, mutually complementary roles to be played by husband and wife. This is to take account of their psychological and physiological specificities, in case of women their unique ability to bear and give life to children. Unless they know already, neuro-biologists may learn from the Qur'an that a **boy is not like a girl** (3: 35).

In accordance with Qur'an and Sunna a Muslim marriage should be based on mutual respect, love, and kindness (30: 21), seeking true equity rather than mere formal *equality*. The couples should be for each other **like a garment** (2: 187). Consequently, husbands do not enjoy a higher *status* than their wives: their duty is to protect them in as much as this is required (4: 34).

When babies are born they are not baptized. Rather, as early as possible, one speaks the call to prayer–containing the *shahada*–into their ears.

Islam permits family planning in order to limit population growth responsibly. Abortion is, however, only allowed if life or health of the mother is at stake. Islamically there is no objection against *in vitro* fertilization with the husband's sperm. Surrogate motherhood is, however, refused by Muslims.

Husband and wife share the duty of educating their offspring. However, mothers have a veto on matters concerning little children and fathers on matters concerning teenagers.

According to the Prophet "divorce is the most detestable of all permitted actions". In case marriage fails, husbands can obtain divorce extrajudicially, by pronouncing it repeatedly. But wives must sue for divorce in a court of law. This figures because they will not have to return their husbands` *mahr* even if the fault for the failure of marriage is entirely theirs (2: 229).

Respect for parents and the elderly is a key Muslim virtue (17: 23 f., 46: 15). They remain integrated into the (extended) family rather than being exiled to old age asylums. The prevailing Western "youth cult" represents the opposite trend.

In case of death, his/her inheritance is split among the surviving spouse and blood relatives of the deceased in a manner regulated by the Qur'an in the greatest detail and therefore hardly amendable by last will dispositions. One consequence of this regime is the inability to keep one`s fortune together, by way of testament, in favor of the oldest (or any other) son.

The Islamic law of inheritance favors sons over their sisters (4: 11, 176). However, after their father`s death sons alone bear the entire responsibility for the financial upkeep of the family.

Islamic divine law, the so-called *shari'ah* , consists mainly of these and other rules of family law and the law of inheritance. These norms codified or not, are still applied in most Muslim countries.

THE MUSLIM STATE

BUILDING BLOCKS

To speak of an Islamic State is misleading because a commonwealth like any incorporated legal personality cannot have a religion. One should rather speak of a Muslim country.

At any rate, the Qur'an knows only of a few building blocks for the construction of a Muslim State. In fact, it does not deal with statehood at all but only with the ideal Muslim community. This implies that there is no Qur'anic necessity of having the monarchies of which most of the Muslim world still is composed. Islamic law only insists on the following:

- The Muslim Ummah should be ruled by a leader (al-amir), i.e. not by committee or politbureau.
- Every single person is a representative of God (al-khalifa) on earth (2: 30; 6: 165; 24: 55).
- Governments must rule on the basis of consultation with the people (ash-shura; 3: 159; 42: 38).
- The judiciary must be independent.

CONSTITUTIONAL SYSTEM

Given the scarcity of norms in matters of State, the Muslims seek guidance for the development of constitutional law (al-ahkam ad-dusturiyya) from the early Muslim conduct of State. The first Muslim community, the Muslim-Jewish confederation of al-Madinah–as of 622 CE–is taken as a model, based as it was on a social contract (al-ba'ia), long before J. J. Rousseau (contrat social) discovered it. Al-Madinah was

- a multi-religious republic
- with a federal structure and
- elected heads of State who were
- both religious and politico-military leaders,
- individually responsible to the people for their conduct.

Against this background more Muslims than ever now see Islam entirely compatible with a republican system of State which is participatory (i.e. democratic), pluralistic, and subject to the rule of law thanks to a division of powers. Consequently, Muslim opposition parties now consider the authoritarian rule in many parts of the Muslim world as downright un-Islamic. That is why Islam is now challenging the political status quo there.

ECONOMIC SYSTEM

As far as the religious foundations of an Islamic economic system (al-ahkam al-iqtisadiyya) are concerned, the normative situation is similar. Qur'an and Sunna provide only a few structural elements, thus allowing a high degree of flexibility.

• The Qur'an presumes a (social) *market economy* and protects *private property* , also as far as the means of production are concerned. Only the airspace, waterways and resources, grazing grounds, forests and minerals are common property. The market is to be protected against manipulation, fraud, monopolies, and cut throat competition.

• Capital must not be invested against fixed returns, commercial interest (ar-riba) being forbidden (2: 275; 3: 130). In other words: Capital can only be used in contractual modes which provide for a sharing of both gains and losses. This is possible not only in (unincorporated) commercial partnerships and companies but also through long-term, non-speculative investing in stocks.

• Insurance on the basis of mutuality, practiced already at the time of the Prophet (s.), is an allowed way of controlling risks.

• Any speculation, be it with money (hedge funds), foreign currencies, or goods (futures) is forbidden, as are lotteries, money wagers and horse or soccer betting.

• Goods and capital must not be hoarded so as to manipulate market prices and exploit shortages in times of crisis like droughts or crop failures (9: 34 f.). At the same time, wastefulness and indulging in luxuries is also considered reprehensible (6: 141; 7: 55;

17: 27). The Islamic law of taxation and inheritance counteracts such behavior by raising taxes on property regardless of income and by distributing estates among many heirs. Both measures ensure a greater degree of money circulation than would be the case otherwise.

• Usury is forbidden, as is the production of goods whose consumption is not allowed (alcoholic drinks; pork; party drugs; outlawed weaponry).

• Prostitution must not become organized or officially recognized (as socially insured, tax paying "sex workers").

It goes without saying that an Islamic economy is to serve people and the common interest, not profiteering, although trading with profit is good and normal. However, on the whole, Islam provides more moral rules for economists than rules for economic theorists.

There is not a single country in existence where the Islamic rules for running the economy have been fully implemented, even though more and more institutes for Islamic banking are being set up, even in London. In particular, Pakistan still struggles with abolishing interest.

ECOLOGY

From a Muslim viewpoint God manifested Himself twofold, both in His universe and in His verbal revelations. This alone should exclude that nature, instead of being treated like a divine trust, is exploited destructively:

Do not spread corruption on earth after it has been so well ordered (7: 56).

Indeed, to take good care of nature and its resources is a form of piety. This includes cleanliness, the opposite of pollution of the environment. Cleanliness according to Muhammad (s.) makes up half of peoples` faith.

In contrast to the Bible, the Qur'an does not encourage man to subdue the earth for himself. On the contrary, people are to utilize their planet responsibly, like–as a trustee–one deals with a usufruct, given in trust. The Qur'an contains dire predictions of the catastrophes which are going to happen to both land and sea if man mismanages the natural resources (30: 41), including acid rain (56: 68-70).

On the whole Islam does, however, not oppose environmental destruction with ecological romanticism, like the Green Parties, but with an appeal to the moral, religious responsibilities of each individual. In short, environmental ethics is part of man's transcendental links.

DEFENSE

A Muslim State is obliged to protect peace by doing what is necessary for assuring its military defense (8: 60). Thus armament is to serve the maintenance of peace and external security through deterrence. Therefore Muslims must positively respond to the draft.

Draft dodging and conscientious objection to the draft are not admitted (2: 216). Defense being a societal duty, the individual Muslim can refuse serving in the armed forces only if enough volunteers are available.

The use of force is restricted by the Qur'an to two cases only:
• defense against an external attack, including pre-emption if an attack is imminent (2: 190; 4: 90; 9: 13; 22: 39; 75: 90 f.)
• resistance against tyrannical despotism (8: 39; 42: 39, 42).

Fighting must be proportionate, not excessive (2: 194; 42: 40), and must stop the moment aggression or tyranny ends (2: 192; 8: 61).

In the course of combat care must be taken not to harm non-combatants (2: 191; 22: 40). This excludes the use of nuclear, chemical and biological weapons of mass destruction. Also willful destruction of the livelihood of the opponent (economic warfare) is not permitted.

The Christian concept of a holy or just war (sacrum bellum, justum bellum) has no equivalent in Islam. On the contrary, the Qur'an forbids any attempt to enforce religious beliefs: **There shall be no coercion in matters of faith** (2: 256). On the contrary, the Qur'an promotes a liberal attitude in religious affairs: **The truth from your Sustainer: Let him who wills, believe in it, and let him who wills, reject it** (18; 29).

It is therefore inappropriate and even misleading to translate *al-jihad* as "holy war". Literally *jihad* rather means "effort", in any area, be it the struggle against one's low instincts or be it armed struggle against an intruder or, as in Palestine, against illegal occupation.

For Muslims, at any rate, the greatest *jihad* is the one for moral perfection.

RELIGIOUS MINORITIES

Islam disapproves of coercion in matters of religion (2: 256) since God has given each people its own way of worship (22: 67). The protection of religious minorities therefore is not only a matter of international law but, for Muslims, a religious duty as well (10: 108; 16: 93; 18: 29).

Originally, these rules safeguarded Jewish, Christian and Sabean religious minorities (adh-dhimmi) called "People of the Book" (ahl al-kitab). Later this protection was extended to Zoroastrians (al-majus) and even to Hindus.

In this field Islamic jurisprudence in its details is largely based on the pre-Islamic customary law of asylum (as-siyar), but also on the liberal Constitution of al-Madinah and a treaty concluded by the Prophet (s.) with the Christian community in the oasis of Najran (631 CE).

The Qur'anic foundation of religious pluralism is best expressed in 5: 48–a veritable manifesto of religious tolerance:

...To every one of you have We appointed a law and way. And if God had so willed, He could have made you one single community. But (He wanted) to test you by what He has given you. Compete, then, with each other in doing good. To God you will all return. Then He will inform you of the things about which you had differed.

Accordingly all non-Muslims, including atheists (9: 6), do not only enjoy the right to practice their religion, even publicly; they are also entitled to manage their own day-to-day affairs autonomously, including family law and the law of inheritance. This arrangement might well be called Pax Islamica. As long as they do not opt for full citizenship, non-Muslims in a Muslim country only pay a "head tax" (jizya) and are exempt from military service.

This then is the foundation of a religious pluralism, laid in the 7th century CE, an attitude (but not yet a legal practice) at long last copied by the Oecumenical movement and its "World Parliament of Religions" in Chicago.

Racial Minorities

The protection of racial minorities in Islam follows the Qur'anic assertion that people must be classed by one criterion only: piety.

We have created you male and female and made you into nations and tribes so that you might come to know each other. The noblest of you in the sight of God is the one who is best in conduct (49: 13).

Islam indeed succeeded better than other religions in eliminating racial discrimination. Muslim countries never knew the kind of racial segregation practiced in South Africa or the United States. If absolute equality is not fully realized in the Muslim world, this is rarely due to skin color.

When Islam was born, slavery was a global phenomenon. Under Roman Law slaves were not even treated as human beings but as mere objects. In contrast, the Qur'an seeks to abolish slavery, step by step, and–for the time being–improved the status of those deplorable people who nevertheless continue to be treated like slaves, be it de iure or de facto, as happened in the Archipelago Gulag and Guantanamo Bay:

- Muslims were forbidden to enslave other Muslims.
- Slaves were given rights, including the right to marry and to ransom themselves. Now their life and inviolability were protected (24: 33).

  Thus slaves in the technical sense could rise to the rank of military commander and even Great Vizier in the Ottoman Empire.
- To free a slave was made a good deed, implying that the very institution of slavery was bound to disappear.

Therefore, Muslim countries without any reservations can ratify international covenants outlawing slavery.

ANIMAL PROTECTION

Muslims are to respect animals as God's co-creation, man and animals essentially being fellow creatures: **There is no animal on earth and no bird flying with its two wings which are not creatures like yourselves** 6: 38). In fact, according to the Qur'an animals, too, are members of an Ummah. Indeed, in Islam kindness to animals has great moral merits. How can one keep fellow creatures, like chickens, in mass cages?

Following their Prophet's (s.) advice and practice, Muslims while giving cats, clean by nature, shelter will not keep dogs, dirty by nature, inside their apartments.

Islam is not a vegetarian religion. It allows the consumption of meat provided that butchering has been conducted in the Islamo-Judaic kosher manner which, if properly conducted, is as "humane" a form of slaughtering as any other.

It is remarkable, though, that the many Qur'anic descriptions of food in paradise, with a single exception, only mention vegetarian dishes.

THEOCRACY OR SECULARISM ?

As we have seen, Islam provides a number of rules for the conduct of State. Even so, a Muslim State need not be a theocracy. After all, only the Prophet Muhammad (s.) was both a binding religious and secular authority. Even before the development of the modern concept of State Muslims used to distinguish between worldly and religious matters (ad-dunya wa-l-akhira), between religion and State (din wa dawla). Thus during the entire Muslim history government (Caliph; Amir; Sultan) on one side and religious authorities ('Ulama; Muftis; Fuqaha) on the other were distinct institutions, often in opposition to each other.

In that sense, Islamic secularism is traditional, not, however, in the sense of French and Mexican laicism. Islam opposes an *elimination* of religion from the public sphere without seeking a *fusion* of State and religion. Rather Islam promotes a harmonious relationship between the two. This may lead to a limited integration of religion into the State, as is the case in Great Britain, Scandinavia, Austria, Spain and Germany. In the Federal Republic this takes the form of religious instruction in public schools, the raising of "church taxes" for officially recognized denominations, the employment of "chaplains" in prisons and the armed forces, the legal protection of religious holidays, and a blasphemy article in the criminal code.

While Islam does not require that governments be composed of clerics, as in the current Iranic Shi'i theocracy, Muslim governments must respect the Qur'anic command to **order what is right and forbid what is wrong** (3: 104, 110, 114; 22: 41), thereby taking account of the *shari'ah*. Any Muslim government will consider the Qur'an as its supreme, constitutional norm.

Islamic Denominations

Defining a Muslim

Now it is possible to define who is a Muslim and who is not:

In a non-historical, timeless, non-denominational sense anybody believing in a single God, conscious of, and obedient to, Him is a Muslim. Abraham was such a Muslim.

In a historical, concrete denominational sense only he / she is a Muslim who pronounces the Islamic confession of faith (ash-shahada), believing in, or respecting, respectively

- God, His angels, His prophets, His books and life after death;
- the Qur'an as God`s authentic, eternal Word;
- Muhammad (s.) as God`s last and final messenger and a beautiful example to be emulated (5: 3; 24: 54; 33: 21);
- the Shari'ah as divine law;
- the Five Pillars of Islam (prayer, fasting, zakat-tax, pilgrimage).

Such a person can call himself a formal Muslim. A Mu`min (faithful) he will, however, only become through interiorization of the contents of his "confession" (49: 14 f.). Therefore nobody should consider himself a Muslim who–like so-called "cultural" or "liberal" Muslims–does not subscribe to the entire religious "package" listed above.

Consequently Turkish and Kurdish Alevites, Syrian Alawites, and Pakistani Qadianis/Ahmadis cannot claim to be Muslims, nor can Turkish Kemalists who admit to no more than "having Allah in their hearts". The Qur'an comments upon their attitude as follows: **There are those among men who worship God only marginally** (22: 11). Every religion has the right to define itself. Nor is it an arrogant exclusivism when Christian Churches refuse, for instance, Jehova`s Witnesses, Mormons, Mennonites or Christian Scientists.

Muslims must, however, absolutely avoid to pass the judgement of disbelief (al-kufr) against someone who claims to believe. Such a judgement presupposes a knowledge of the forum internum to which God alone has access.

It is different in case a Muslim himself declares his apostasy (ar-ridda). To reject Islam (al-irtidad) is, however, not subject to any punishment in this world, unless it translates into hostile activity against Islam. In that eventuality apostasy as high treason becomes a crime punishable in all systems of law.

SHI'ITE ISLAM

Very soon after the death of the Prophet (s.) the Muslim community split into "Sunni" majority Islam and the Party (Shi'a) of 'Ali b. Abu Talib, the Prophet's (s.) valiant cousin and son-in-law. The issue was political: Succession. 'Ali unsuccessfully claimed the office of Caliph for himself on the ground that he was a close member of the Prophet's family. Forestalling a development into monarchy the majority three times in a row chose caliphs who were friends, but no blood relatives, of the Prophet (s.): Abu Bakr (d.634), 'Umar (d. 644) and 'Uthman (d. 656). When 'Ali, at long last, became the 4th caliph he had to face nothing but revolt and was murdered in 661.

As a result of this political dispute the Muslim world is still divided into Sunnis and Shi'is, much like the Christian world is split into Catholics and Protestants. Shi'a Islam is found mainly in Iran, Iraq, the Lebanon, Bahrain and a Northern province of Saudi Arabia.

The Shi'a, in turn, split into majority "Twelver Shi'a" and the minoritarian "Sevener Shi'a" in addition to a "Fiver Shi'a", found in Yemen. Twelver Shi'a (ithna-'ashariyya) is set apart from Sunni Islam as follows:

- Refusal to recognize the legitimacy of the first three caliphs.
- Rejection of all Prophetic traditions (ahadith) transmitted by these three and by 'A'isha, Muhammad's (s.) favorite wife.
- Belief in the inerrancy and esoteric understanding of the Qur'an of the 12 Shi'i caliphs, all descendants of the Prophet (s.).

- Expectation that the last of these, Muhammad al-Muntazar, disappeared in 874 CE and since then living in hiding (al-ghayb), will return as a sort of savior at the end of days.
- Veneration of 'Ali as God's Friend (wali Allah).
- Dramatic mourning for Hussain, son of 'Ali, who was killed near Kerbala, in 680, when claiming the office of khalif (veritable mar tyrdom cult) .
- Permission to dissimulate one's Shi'a affiliation (at-taqiyya) and to conclude temporary marriages (al- mut'a).

In addition one runs into theologically less important, more atmospheric differences setting Sunni and Shi'i Muslims apart. What counts is, however, that the latter accept, and fulfill, all conditions for being Muslims listed in the previous chapter. Therefore, they represent a non-heterodox trend within Islam. This is even more true of the Zayidi (Fiver) Muslims in the Yemen and the 'Ibadi Muslims in 'Uman.

Serious doubts about their relationship to authentic Islam are, however, justified with regard to the secretive, esoteric and gnostic Sevener (Ismaili) Muslims and the sectarian and eclectic Lebanese Druzes.

ISLAMIC HISTORY

EARLY EXPANSION

The political and the religious history of the Muslim world is fascinating. This is already true for the first epoch, the era of the Rightly Guided Caliphs (al-khulafa ar-rashidun) on which we are informed in the greatest detail thanks to the Islamic science of Prophetic and other traditions.

Parallel to the large collections of ahadith, the first biographies (as-siyar) of the Prophet were written by Muhammad ibn Ishaq (d. 767) and at-Tabari (d. 923), also the first Qur'an commentator. The biographers were noticeably less scrupulous in sifting their material for spurious reports than the Hadith-scientists. The latter were of course conscious of the fact that their scrutiny was of crucial importance for the development of Islamic jurisprudence. Given this background and the fact that some 400 letters by the Prophet have been preserved, his personality and activity is historically authenticated like no other figure's in late antiquity.

Fascinating, in particular, is the explosive expansion of Islam immediately after the Prophet's (d.) death, still seen as miraculous, as one country after the other accepted Islam:

- 636 Syria
- 641 Egypt
- 642 Persia.

In addition, in

- 674 siege was laid to Constantinople
- 711 Muslims crossed over into Spain,
- 732 reaching Tours and Poitiers in Central France.

Thus, within a century, Islam spread from Arabia to the Atlantic and Central Europe, pushed the Byzantine Empire back to Anatolia, and simultaneously reached Central Asia via Persia. This military success must be attributed to some degree to the courage and zeal of the Muslim fighters who in their thirst for paradise via martyrdom not only disdained, but actually sought, death.

But bravery alone does not account for the expansion of the new religion, neither its speed nor its extent. The biggest army which the Muslims had been able to field during the lifetime of the Prophet (s.) counted 12. 000 warriors (Battle of Hunayn). Regardless of religious devotion, with such a small contingent—in tune with the limited human and economic resources of Arabia—no world empire could have been conquered.

Indeed, the formidable early outreach of Islam was mainly due to the fact that the populations in the Near and Middle East, Iran, Egypt, North Africa, and Spain accepted this religion with open arms, because

- Muslims were more tolerant than Christians towards minorities and their religions;
- the Islamic law of taxation and its application was milder than the Byzantine equivalents;
- many Oriental Christians and those in Spain as followers of Arianism, as Nestorians or Donatists were heterodox in not believing in Trinity, i.e. the divinity of Jesus as defined by Rome; in particular, the Visigoths in Andalusia and the Vandals in (today's) Algeria had always seen Jesus as a prophet, like the Muslims;
- the Islamic creed was much simpler than the Christian one (: no Original Sin; no Salvation on the Cross; no Holy Ghost; no Sacraments);
- Islam as religion of the middle way (al-wasatiyya), giving its due to this world and the next, was preferred to the world-denying ascetic and monkish interpretation of Christianity, especially by Copts.

At any rate, the Muslim armies never fought against populations as such.

Different from Athens and Rome, Muslim cities were not built by slaves. Also the famous antique library of Alexandria was never burned by Muslims. Indeed, Islam never spread thanks to "Fire and the Sword" as is still claimed. It spread thanks to its attractiveness both as religion and civilization.

CALIPHATE OF DAMASCUS AND BAGHDAD

After the death of 'Ali and the chaos following it the office of caliph was transferred, at least *de facto*, to Damascus and held by the very Umayyad family who, in Mecca, had been Muhammad`s (s.) worst enemies.

No wonder, the Umayyad khulafa were more known for their luxuries, despotism and worldly interests than for piety.

The resentment against this turn of affairs was exploited by another famous Meccan dynasty, the Abbasids, including the family of the Prophet. In 750 CE they managed to overthrow the Umayyades and found a new Muslim empire ruled, for 500 years to come, from Baghdad. This of all cities was turned into a fairy tale residence, still associated with Harun ar-Rashid and the narratives of "1001 Nights". In fact, Baghdad became the most civilized and busiest cultural and scientific metropolis of the Middle Ages, without any equivalent in the Occident except Cordoba in Muslim Spain. Philosophy, theology, law, medicine, all other sciences, poetry, music, falconry, and fashion –all were at home in Baghdad.

PHILOSOPHICAL DISPUTES

Baghdad is not only remembered as birth place of systematic Islamic theology (al-kalam) but also as the site of the first philosophical dispute within Islam. This controversy was consequence of a Hellenization of Islamic thought introduced by philosophers like al-Kindi (d. 873) and Ibn Farabi (d. 950). In particular the study of Aristotle had led to the creation of the Mu`tazila, a rationalistic school of thought that measured the Qur'anic revelation against human reason rather than considering it as the handmaiden of religion. Mu`tazili thinkers defended the following positions:

- Eternity of the universe
- Creator of the Qur'an (khalq al-Qur'an)

- Free Will
- God's attributes being allegorical

These teachings, singly and in sum, were considered heretical by those fundamentalist Muslims who as followers of Ibn Hanbal only accepted Qur'an and Sunna for every issue (Ahl al-kitab wa-s-Sunna).

Had God not anticipated the Mu'tazili way of thinking ? :...**the false beliefs which they invent cause them to betray their faith** (3: 24).

Resistance against giving reason priority over revelation led to the formation of a counter-philosophical school which set out to beat the Mu'tazila with its own methods. This movement crystallized around Abu-l-Hasan al-Ash'ari (d. 941) whose school would later culminate in the greatest Muslim philosophical mind ever, Abu Hamid al-Ghazali (d. 1111).

The Ash'arites taught
- Finality of the Universe
- Authenticity of the Qur'an
- Predetermination to a large degree (taqdir)
- Belief in revelation "without asking how?" (bi-la kaifa)
- Refusal of metaphysical speculation, i.e. **attributing to God that which they do not know** (7: 33).

In Baghdad philosophical disputes could turn into political strife. From time to time, one of the caliphs interfered in favor of one of the schools or, on the contrary, proscribed it under penalty. In the long run, it was al-Ash'ari and al-Ghasali who won by developing a critique of human perception which pre-dated the one by Immanuel Kant and Ludwig Wittgenstein by 750 to 950 years. Thus, Islamic philosophy incriminated philosophical speculation and ended metaphysics way ahead of similar intellectual developments in the Occident. Since then one may still talk about Muslim philosophers but no longer of Islamic philosophy.

This turn of Muslim orthodoxy corresponded in fact with those Qur'anic passages that deal with scientific theory like 6: 99, 29: 24 and 10: 10. These verses tell us that observing the signs of God in nature is of use only for those who already believe in God and is useless for disbelievers. In other words: According to the Qur'an faith precedes knowledge. Knowledge does not engender faith but only confirms it.

People aware of the philosophical trajectory of Martin Heidegger will immediately understand these bizarre sounding allegations. Post-modern (no longer Cartesian) philosophers know that people only see what they wish to see or what they merely perceive thanks to their social impregnation. We can indeed pose questions. But we can only formulate questions allowed, or provoked by, our cultural embedding.

This was common wisdom among Muslims in Baghdad, nine centuries ago.

ANDALUSIA

One single Umayyad prince managed to escape to the Muslim Far West (al-maghrib) when his family was massacred during the Abbasid revolution in 750 CE. His most famous descendant, 'Abd ar-Rahman III (d.961), set himself up as Umayyad counter-caliph in exile and turned his capital, Cordoba (Andalusia) into the most developed cultural center of its time in Europe. Andalusia–Sevilla, Murcia, Toledo, Salamanca, Granada, Cordoba–under the Muslims achieved a cultural symbiosis between Jews, Christians, and Muslims never seen before or after. In fact, in spite of many short-comings of a political nature, the Golden Age of Muslim Spain to this day nourishes Muslim pride and nostalgia. Tourists flocking to the Great Mosque in Cordoba, the Giralda minaret in Sevilla, and the Alhambra Castle above Granada get a glimpse of this past glory.

No surprise that Andalusia then was home to intellectual giants like Ibn Rushd (d. 1198), the philosopher-jurist known in the West as Averroës; Ibn Hazm (d. 1064), founder of a school of jurisprudence and also excelling in logic, psychology and aesthetics; Ibn Tufayl (d. 1185), as a fore-runner of Jostein Gardener author of the first philosophical novel (Hayy ibn Yaqsan); and Ibn 'Arabi (d. 1240), already encountered as greatest speculative mystic ever.

Via Ibn Rushd`s commentaries Western Europe re-discovered Aristotelian philosophy and the decisive impulses for the development of Scholasticism. Ibn Hazm`s love lyrics helped inspiring Troubadour singers in the Provence region of southern France. Ibn 'Arabi found some his most faithful followers among Catholic mystics and is still studied by 'Ibn Arabi societies in Britain and France. With his novel, Ibn Tufayl provided the scheme for "Robinson Crusoe". The Gothic arches of churches in the West are a reminder of Muslim Andalusia as well.

From there the Indian-Arabic numerals, including the all important zero, invaded Western bookkeeping, freeing it at long last from the cumbersome Roman system of numerals (without zero). It was Muslim channels, too, through which the Occident received the sciences of arithmetic, algebra, artillery, astronomy, botany, chemistry, epidemiology, hygiene, optics, paper-making, surgery, and trigonometry. The medical text-book by Ibn Sina (a.k.a. Avicenna), his famous *Qanun*, until the end of the 16th century had already seen 16 editions in the Occident.

Thus it was predictable that the first translation into a Western language–Latin–of the Qur'an would be produced in Andalusia (Toledo, 1143).

After 800 years, Muslim Andalusia, weakened by disunity and a permanent conflict between Arab and Berber Muslims, came to a tragic end in 1492 when its last stronghold, Granada, fell to fanatical Catholic invaders. In violation of written promises, this "Reconquista" culminated in the expulsion of virtually all Muslims and Jews, as from 1608. (An early case of "ethnic cleansing".) The latter fled into Muslim areas like North Africa (Fes), Greece (Saloniki), and Turkey (Istanbul). Reconquista was of course a misnomer because before the 15th century Andalusia had never been Catholic.

CRUSADES AND MONGOLIAN CONQUESTS

Catholic offensives had similarly catastrophic results in the Muslim east. First British, German and French Christian knights during a series of Crusades fought their way into the Near East, in 1204 plundering Constantinople as well, for them a heretical (Greek-

Orthodox) metropolis.

After butchering, in 1099, the entire population of Jerusalem in one of the worst massacres ever recorded, the Knights installed themselves for exactly 200 years in what today is south-eastern Anatolia, Lebanon, Syria, Palestine, and Jordan. Their military superiority was, however, not matched by their civility, level of education, or standard of life. For the Muslims the Crusaders were barbarians who had much to learn, not only in terms of hygiene and medicine but also in tolerance and honesty. His moral superiority turned the Kurdish liberator of Palestine, Salah ad-Din al-Ayubi (d. 1193), into an Occidental legend as well ("Saladin").

Parallel to the Crusades the Muslim east fell victim to another catastrophe, the Mongol invasion. In 1258, under Hulagu Khan, grandson of Jenghiz Khan, they killed the last Abbasid caliph in Baghdad, terminating both a great empire and a brilliant civilization.

But then the most unexpected happened: The conquerors within a very short time adopted Islam, the religion of the conquered.

The same had happened before to the Turkish soldiers, recruited by the caliphs in Baghdad. They, now as Mamluks in Egypt, were the only ones who could match the Mongols in the field. In 1260, at the 'Ayn Jalut river, the Mamluks inflicted on them their first and only defeat. Now Cairo became the central city of Islam.

THE OTTOMAN EMPIRE

Conquering first Anatolia and Thrace, then Constantinople (1453) and finally Egypt (1517), the Ottoman Turks imposed themselves as the protective power of Islam. Sultan Selim I now made Istanbul the fifth (and last) seat of caliphs. Under his successor, Süleyman Qanuni (the "Law giver"), reigning from 1520 to1566, the Ottoman Empire already reached its golden age and zenith, symbolized by magnificent mosques built by his architect Sinan in Edirne (Selimiye cami) and Istanbul (Süleymaniye cami).

Now, for the second time, Europe became mortally afraid of Islam, as the Ottomans occupied the Balkans and even laid siege twice to Vienna, the Hapsburg Imperial capital (1529; 1683).

Decline and Colonization

Gradually the balance of power turned against the Ottomans. This trend became first manifest during the naval battle at Lepanto, in 1572, a disaster for them. After the second failure to take Vienna, decadence set in for which the18th century Ottoman craze for tulips was symptomatic.

When Europe in the 19th century embarked on colonizing the world, Turkey was of no help. It barely could prevent being colonized itself, by Greece after World War I.

Napoleon I with his "expedition" to Egypt (1798-1801) opened the rush.

Soon, the entire Muslim world except central Arabia and Turkey proper was in the hands of British, Dutch, French and Russian colonists, from Morocco to India and Indonesia to Kazahstan. Following in the footsteps of Napoleon, the German Emperor William II as well, in Tanger, Jerusalem and Istanbul, posed as self-appointed "protector of Islam".

Now Western people discovered key examples of Islamic art, like the Taj Mahal in Agra, the Red Fort in Delhi, the Kutubiyya in Marrakesh, the venerable mosques in Kairouan and Cairo (Ibn Tulun). But they failed to discover the spirituality which had informed the aesthetics of such buildings. Thus the Occident ruled, but did not understand, the Orient.

ISLAM TODAY

INDEPENDENCE

Under Shaykh 'Abd al-Qadir (Abdelkader) the Algerians fought well but desperately and, in the long run, without chances of success against the French intruders, as from 1830. Nor could the Sudanese Mahdi when revolting in 1885 hope to succeed militarily against the British in spite of his initial triumph at Khartoum. However, both inspired the liberation movements which regained independence for the Muslim world, mostly in bloody struggles as in Algeria (1954-1962).

Yet this was not the end of the colonial trauma. It now proved extremely detrimental that the colonial powers following a policy of Christianization and de-Islamization had formed local elites in their own image. Therefore most of the first generation post-colonial leaders in the Muslim world, like Ben Bella, Bourgiba, Gamal'Abd an-Nassr, Sœkarno, and Jinnah, were Muslims mainly by name and followed socialist, nationalist or corrupt despotic policies. Thus Islam only came to the fore after these ideologies had proven disastrous, perpetuating the under-developed Third World status of most Muslim countries.

This is the background of much of the rhetoric of the opposition-al Islamic Movement ("Islam is the solution"; "The Qur'an is our constitution"). Many of its older members had belonged to Islamically motivated groups which had put up anti-colonial resistance.

ORIENTALISM

As early as during the 18th century there were a number of enlightened minds who studied as much of Islam as they could get hold of, with sympathy and even empathy. Among them, in Germany, Johann Jakob Reiske, King Frederic the Great of Prussia, Gotthold E. Lessing, and Johann Wolfgang von Goethe. Germany not being a classical colonial power, German orientalists were less likely than their colleagues in Britain, France, and the Netherlands to become agents of colonization. Rather,

German orientalists became renowned for their scientific depth and relative objectivity, whether they coped with the Qur'an (Heinrich L. Fleischer, d. 1888; Rudi Paret, d. 1983), Islamic history (Theodor Nöldeke, d. 1930), prophetic traditions (Ignaz Goldziher, d. 1921), Islamic law (Josef Schacht, d. 1969), Muslim literature (Carl Brockelmann, d. 1956), and Sufis (Hellmut Ritter, d. 1971; Annemarie Schimmel, d. 2003).

Simultaneously, orientalism in Great Britain, France and the Netherlands withe few exceptions developed into an after-science of colonialism.

Typically, Arab and Islam experts like Lawrence of Arabia and Harry St. John Philby were also secret agents. Edward Said, a Christian Palestinian, was therefore justified in portraying much of British, French and Dutch orientalism as a projection of European prejudices onto an Orient invented by them ("Orientalism", 1978). Islamology still suffers from his verdict.

THE ISLAMIC MOVEMENT
Phenomenon of Modernity

Muslim history has always known periodic attempts to reform the practice of Islam by re-establishing and defending the pristine faith as it had been taught and lived in al-Madinah. Muslims even believed that every century would see a particular charismatic "renewer" (al-mujadid) of Islam. Today, the Islamic Movement (al-harakat al-islamiyya) is fulfilling this function. One of its best known leaders, the Pakistani Khurram Murad (d.1997) outlined its purpose as follows: "Organized efforts to transform the existing society into an Islamic one, based on Qur'an and Sunna, so that Islam becomes the supreme guidance for putting all aspects of life into order..."

Accordingly, the Islamic Movement is well anchored in the past. At the same time, however, it is a thoroughly modern phenomenon as far as its methodology and its lay leadership is concerned. The Islamic Movement does not seek to modernize Islam but to Islamize modernity. But it operates competently within that modernity.

The Islamic Movement in spite of its many doctrinal and national shadings, was undoubtedly the most important factor for the totally unexpected revitalization (an-nahda) and re-awakening (as-sahwa) of Islam in the 20th century.

Within the Muslim world the Movement acts as a religious socio-political protest organization against the un-Islamic status quo. There it mainly attracts the rural population, urban proletariat, students and intellectuals and lower ranks within police and militia.

Outside the Muslim world the Movement rather acts as a pietistic socio-political organization serving the preservation of an Islamic identity abroad.

BIRTH CONDITIONS

After the 15th century the Muslim world had virtually lost its ability to renew itself and to cope with emerging challenges. That is how it became colonizable, and promptly was colonized. The Muslim world did not become decadent because it was colonized. Rather it was colonized because it had been decadent. The Westernization that followed, going hand in hand with colonization, threatened to marginalize Islam to the point of becoming extinct.

This situation alarmed Muslims who were alert to what happened around them, in particular Shah Wali Allah (d. 1763) in India and Muhammad ibn 'Abd al-Wahhab (d. 1787) in Arabia. In the 19th century these isolated beacons of light were strengthened by early reformers, in particular Jamal ad-Din al-Afghani (d. 1897), a political genius, and Shaykh Muhammad Abduh (d. 1905), the sophisticated and influential rector of the al-Azhar University in Cairo. On this basis, in 1928, Hassan al-Banna, an Egyptian school teacher, founded the by now legendary Muslim Brothers (al-ikhwan al-muslimun) and,1941in India, Abu-l-'Ala al-Mawdudi the corresponding *Jama'at al-Islami*: Both are the prototypes of most current groups within the Islamic Movement, like ABIM and *Al-Arqam* in Malaysia, *Nahdatul Ulema* in Indonesia, *Jama'at at-Tabligh*, founded in Bangladesh, Shaykh

Ahmed Yassin`s *Hamas* in Palestine, the *Takhrik-e-Islami* in Pakistan, M.T.I. and *an-Nahda* in Tunisia, the F.I.S. and *Hamas* in Algeria, *Milli Görüs* in Turkey, and *Hizbullah* in the Lebanon.

All these are highly motivated and organized lay formations with an extremely high percentage of academically trained members. For a long time, but no longer, Sayyid Qutb`s book "Milestones" (1964) served as their manifesto.

It is therefore a mistake to label "bread revolts" what in fact was an uprising of Muslim youths against corrupt or incapable governments. They wanted bread and butter, yes, but also a less trivial thing: Islam.

THE CONTEMPORARY SCENE

The Islamic Movement in less than a century succeeded in bringing about in the Muslim world a moral re-armament and an Ummatic feeling of togetherness as well as a political consciousness absent before. In the process, the Movement through its intimate contact with the West shed much of its earlier combatant authoritarianism, turning into a democratic alternative to the status quo in the Muslim world.

Young Muslim Militants are frequently called "Islamists" (instead of "fundamentalists" formerly); some call themselves this way. This suggests a uniquely Muslim phenomenon. (Fundamentalists one can find among Jews, Zionists, and Christians as well!) It also suggests that Islam, for them, was not a religion but merely a political *ideology*.

"Islamism" is a misnomer because it is a command of Islam and a duty of all Muslims to bring their religious conviction to bear in the public sphere, just as Catholics and Jews do it.

Unfortunately, there are indeed a few but vocal and attention seeking Muslims who tend to reduce their religion to political concerns. Some—the *Hizb at-Tahrir* (Liberation Party)—are obsessed with just one aim: To re-establish the office of caliph, abolished by Mustafa Kemal in 1924. Others became so sectarian that they commit the grave sin of monopolizing Islam for themselves and excommunicating other Muslims (at-takfir).

PROCLIVITY TO VIOLENCE?

Islam permits armed resistance against illegal suppression (al-zulm) by tyrannical regimes (42: 41 f.). But it is not wise or opportune, respectively, always to do what one is entitled to do. Rather one has to take into account the chances of success and the risks for innocent others.

Yet, in spite of the most uneven odds, Muslims of a radical mindset are frequently deciding to fight illegitimate but extremely powerful regimes and to resort to un-Islamic methods of warfare, like kidnapping, suicide bombing, and large scale killing of non-combatants, in order to make up for their military inferiority.

This leads the media to report on "Islamic terrorism" even though Islam and terrorism are incompatible. 'Usama bin Laden's al-Qa'ida organization and its large scale attacks, like on 11 September 2001 in New York and on 11 March 2004 in Madrid, have hurt the image of Islam world-wide more than anything else since the time of the Assassins in the 12th / 13th century.

This is not to say that angry Muslims are not really suffering from persecution and injustice, in Kashmir, Chechnya, Algeria, and proto-typically in Palestine. Nor can it be denied that the United States is partner to the daily atrocities committed by Israel against Palestinians. Nor should one overlook that prisons in many parts of the Muslim world are over-crowded with committed, mostly peaceful Muslims: Because Islamic political parties if admitted would win free and fair elections in virtually every single Muslim country today. Alas, Western governments, too, show an interest in not allowing such elections because their fear of Islam is greater than their love for democracy in the Third World.

It is absurd: Muslims seeking political asylum in the Occident and learning there the blessings of republicanism, political participation, the rule of law, division of powers, political alternation through honest elections, political control of the military, absolute proscription of torture, freedom of the press, etc., are to forget all that when returning home, for the sake of "stability" and "predictability", in particular as far as the price of oil and gas is concerned.

Does democracy have blue eyes and blond hair? That is the question.

ISLAMOPHOBIA

K. J. Kuschel drew attention to the fact that Europe was currently going through its third wave of pluralism:

In the 16th century the Catholic Church broke apart into a multitude of Christian sects.

In the 18th century, the Christian world opened up to Non-Christians, including deists, atheists and secularists.

Now, since the 20th century, Islam is entering the scene, challenging the basic assumptions of both Christianity *and* Secularism.

This new pluralism did, however, not yet lead to a recognition of the Islamic contribution to what in effect is a Judeo-Christian-Islamic-Hellenistic-Humanist civilization. Rather, the growing visibility of Islam in the West increasingly produced allergic reaction against it.

This explains the popularity of Samuel Huntington's thesis of a "clash of civilization", even though clashes do not take place *between* cultures–they interpenetrate and fertilize each other–but *within* civilizations, as currently in Turkey, Algeria, Israel, Northern Ireland, and the United States.

All over Europe, and now in the United States as well, Muslims live under general suspicion. Thus the essentialist sin is committed to treat Muslims as the "other", each of whom is totally different, being totally motivated by his religion. This perversion is of course politically convenient: By labeling Palestinian or Chechnyan freedom fighters "Islamists", one is excused from dealing with the historical, social, economic, and psychological causes of their actions. In other words: Essentializing a Muslim's behavior safely turns the attention away from contributing causes like Israeli or Russian, Indian or Algerian State terrorism.

It looks as if Islam after the disappearance of the Soviet Union and the Communist threat had resumed its important earlier function as the enemy that helps Europe preserve its threatened identity.

Alas, like all enemy images, Islamophobia is a construct which filters perception by painting over positive aspects of Islam. In this way Islamophobia becomes self-perpetuating. Most likely, the Turkish wish to accede to the European Union will become victim of this mechanism. Indeed, the feared Islamization of the Turkish immigrant population in Germany is not a cause of German anti-Islamic anti-Semitism but a result of it.

MUSLIM-CHRISTIAN DIALOGUE

So much more a dialogue (al-hiwar) is necessary between Muslims and Christians in Europe and North America. Conditions are ripe for it since the Christian churches no longer pursue their missionary efforts under the protection of bayonets.

The Muslims, too, are called on by the Qur'an to invite to Islam (ad-da'wa) in the most friendly and kind manner only (16: 125; 29: 46).

These are better conditions for mutual understanding than ever before.

In the Middle Ages Muslim-Christian encounters were without chance, as proven by the failed attempts of Raymundus Lullus, St. Francis of Assisi, and Emperor Frederic II. No wonder: At that time, the Muslims still divided the world into two halves, the world of Islam (dar al-Islam) and the world of war (dar al-harb)–un-Qur'anic and today obsolete concepts.

Of course, today as well, dialogue is only promising if conducted between equals who do not seek to convert one another, and if one concentrates on social issues rather than engaging in dogmatic disputes. Christian theology certainly is in crisis. Nevertheless, for the time being only a handful of Christian theologians, like John Hick, Hans Küng, Paul Schwarzenau and Gerd Lüdemann, could agree with Muslims on the nature of Jesus (s.) as a prophet, the prophetic role of Muhammad (s.) and the Qur'an as divine revelation.

So it is better to leave these matters alone.

The Catholic Church during the 2nd Vatican Council (1962-65) with its encyclical letter *Pacem in Terris* (Peace in the World; 1963) dropped its fateful doctrine of *extra ecclesiam nulla salus* (no salvation outside of the Church) which had justified so much violence against "heathens" in the past. Also, in its encyclical letter *Nostram Aetate* (In our Age) the Pope expressed the Catholics` high esteem for the Muslims "who worship the One God." But the Vatican managed even then to escape a formal recognition both of Muhammad (s.) as a prophet and the Qur'an as a revelation.

Defective, too, was the rather abstract admission of Christian guilt by Pope John Paul II, in 2002, since he failed to include the Church in his excuses and to call by name the Crusades, the Reconquista, the Inquisition, and the expulsion of the Muslims from Spain.

Before 9/11 the Protestant churches were more forth-coming than their Catholic colleagues in the frame-work of Muslim-Christian dialogues. Now both denominations seem to have gotten cold feet, even showing themselves openly critical of Muslims and their activities.

Even so, gradually the insight is growing that all believers in this world are sitting in one and the same boat, in a growing ocean of disbelief. This should promote a Jewish-Christian-Muslim trialogue as well, provided that the Jewish representatives accept that anti-Zionism is permissible and not to be confused with anti-Semitism.

ISLAMIC INSTITUTIONS AND SYMBOLS

THE CALIPHATE

In the very beginning, the office of caliph as the only Islamic institution was in charge of all worldly and religious affairs of the Muslim community. Seat of the caliphs until 656 was al-Madinah, then shortly Kufa, followed from 661-750 by Damascus (ash-Sham) and from 750-1258 by Baghdad. After this city "built in the round" the caliphs were at home in Cairo until 1517 and, finally, in Istanbul. On 3 March, 1924, Mustafa Kemal abolished this glorious institution which had existed for 1292 years. The last caliph, Abdülmecit II ('Abd al-Majid II) died in Paris, in 1944. From time to time, the Muslims had been able to choose between two rival caliphs, like the Abbasid one in Baghdad and the Umayyad one in Cordoba. But they had never experienced a time *without* any *Shaykhu-l-Islam*.

The new situation came as a shock, leading to considerable consternation in India. In fact, several serious attempts were made to re-create the office of caliph. Alas, King Faisal of Saudi Arabia refused the offer to serve as caliph, and the hope to set up the Organization of the Islamic Conference as multilateral, institutional caliphate came to naught. Today, only the *Hizb at-Takhrir* organization, founded in 1952 by the Jordanian Shaykh Taqi ad-Din al-Nabhani, actively dreams of a re-creation of this office.

In contrast, main-stream Muslims agree with the view already held by Shaykh Ibn Taymiyya, 14th century anti-Sufi reform theologian, that if need be the Muslims can do without a *caliph* but certainly not without the *shari'ah*. He had gained this conviction when witnessing the consequences of the Mongol conquest which had deprived the Muslims of a caliph for the first time. At any rate, the current Muslim call for implementation of the *shari'ah* is sounded much louder than the one for finding a new caliph.

FUNCTIONARIES

The Muslim world is relatively poor in terms of institutions. This may be due to the fact that it is not organized like a church and does not know of sacraments which require administration by a an ordained clergy like priests or bishops. On the contrary, every single Muslim as a viceregent of God is a religiously autonomous individual with direct access to all acts of worship. This empowerment jibes with the Muslims` belief that intercession with God in behalf of someone else–and be it by a "Mother of God", a saint or a priest–is theologically impossible. Everyone is responsible (only) for himself and stands in front of God, directly and alone.

Therefore, Islam only knows of a few religious *professions*: *Imams* who lead the ritual prayer in the mosque and as preachers (al-khuta-ba; sing. al-khatib) deliver the Friday sermon (al-khutba); *Muezzins* who call for prayer; and *Muftis* who issue legal opinions (al-fatawa; sing. al-fatwa).

Nor did the Muslim world develop a large number of religious *insti-tutions*: The (neighborhood) *mosque* (al-masjid) and the central (Friday prayer) mosque (al-jam´i); religious *schools* (al-madaris, sing. al-madrasa; and charitable *foundations* (al-awqaf; sing. al-waqf) - most of them run privately.

Even Islamic jurisprudence was developed privately, i.e. by independ-ent *scholars* (al-fuqaha, sing. al-faqih) whose authority solely stood on their personal prestige.

AN ISLAMIC VATICAN ?

It would be absurd to search for an Islamic equivalent to the Pope. True, the ruler of Saudi Arabia recently assumed the title of "Protector of the Two Inviolable Mosques", referring to the one in "noble Mecca" (Makkah al-mukarrama) and the one in "enlight-ened Madina" (Madinah al-Munawwara).However, the Saudi king thereby assumed duties only, without obtaining privileges.

Also the famed old university al-Azhar in Cairo does not confer upon its president, known as Grand Shaykh al-Azhar, any superior status. His authority ends exactly where his personal prestige as a scholar and moral leader ends.

INTERNATIONAL ORGANIZATIONS

The most important Muslim multilateral State organization, founded in 1969 in Rabat, is the Organization of the Islamic Conference/ O.I.C. (Munazama al-Mu`tamar al-Islami) residing in Jiddah. It was created in reaction to a Zionist attempt to burn down the al-Aqsa Mosque in Jerusalem (al-Quds). The O.I.C. is a regional governmental organization of the United Nations. Its own sub-structure includes ISESCO in Rabat, the Muslim equivalent to UNESCO; the Research Center for Islamic History, Art and Culture in Istanbul (IRCICA), the Islamic Development Bank in Jiddah (IDB); the Academy for Islamic Jurisprudence in Mecca; and an Islamic Court and Medical Association, both in Kuwait.

O.I.C. Secretary General, as from 2005, is Prof. Dr. Ekemeleddin Ihsanoglu.

It would be too flattering to claim that O.I.C. has been a success so far. All too often the Palestine conflict leads to internal stalemate. Even so, the O.I.C. has been more effective as an international representation of the Muslim world than the more restricted Arab League.

Among non-governmental Muslim organizations it is worth-while mentioning the Islamic World Congress (al-mu`tamar al-'alami al-islami), operating from Jiddah; it supports Muslim minorities worldwide.

ISLAMIC ORGANIZATIONS IN EUROPE AND NORTH AMERICA

Currently about 30 million Muslims live in Europe. Those in Eastern Europe–Albanians (Arnavut), Bosnians, Tartars–have been around for centuries. Those in Western Europe, approximately 15 million, came recently, mainly as "guest workers" from the Indian subcontinent (to Great Britain), North Africa (to France) and Turkey (to Germany).

Until now, they have been organizing themselves mainly according to national and language criteria, in the case of Turkish immigrants also according to party and sectarian lines. Therefore, Muslims in Europe have not yet arrived anywhere at forming a common central representation. Rather national governments can, and do, set competing Muslim umbrella organizations against each other.

The "Islamic Co-operation Council" in Strasbourg is the (still feeble) attempt to act as a unit within the European Union. This cooperation is hampered by the fact that every member of the European Community has its own laws concerning religious affairs. France is the only country among them not only practicing laïcité but also laïcisme , i.e. the separation of State and religion as a militant ideology. At the other end of the spectrum we find Austria which since 1908 has been dealing with Islam as an officially recognized religion. In Britain, four Muslims have already been appointed to the House of Lords, including Lord Amir Bathia and Lord Nazir Ahmed of Rotherham. Germany, in turn, sports an "Islamic Newspaper" proper, published in Berlin. Britain has a "Muslim life style Magazine" (Emel) and a Muslim academic institution, MIHE, serving as faculty of Islamology of the University of Loughburrough. In France one even finds a regular Sunday morning Islamic TV program.

In view of all this, Islam may be much more visible in Europe now than 30 years ago. Alas, in reaction Islamophobia, too, grew correspondingly.

Muslim efforts run into more, rather than less, difficulties, whether they wish to build mosques (not only behind the railroad tracks), have proper Islamic religious instruction in school, protect the right of Muslim women to dress themselves as modestly as they want, slaughter in halal fashion or bury their dead as Islamically required.

This situation is worsened by the observation that Western media regularly pronounce themselves on Islamic issues without sufficient expert knowledge. Indeed, too many people speak about Islam and Muslims rather than with them. At times, Muslims wonder whether anti-Arab and Muslim anti-Semitism have not taken the place of anti-Jewish anti-Semitism.

The situation of Muslims in the United States for a variety of reasons is markedly different. Having given asylum to so many people persecuted for religious reasons in the Old Continent, America is generally more tolerant towards religious diversity in spite of the fact (or because of it?) that in North America religion plays a greater public role than in Europe.

Of course, it would be highly incorrect politically to invite any of the two million African-American Muslims "to go home". Thanks to them, Islam is indeed indigenous.

However, the majority of American Muslims came from India and Pakistan as well as from the entire Arabic world. But they do not suffer from the stigma of structurally underprivileged guest workers. On the contrary, since most American Muslim immigrants came as students, they form the most affluent part of the Ummah. In fact, one out of 10 medical doctors in the United States is a Muslim. (Doctors there easily become millionaires.)

New York, Washington, Chicago, and Los Angeles are the centers of Muslim activity in the New World. But all over the country one finds Islamic Centers and more than 300 privately run Muslim schools. The US Armed Forces employ Muslims "chaplains" and permit female Muslim soldiers to wear *hijab*. Muslim representatives have been invited to the White House for end-of-Ramadan dinners and to national party conventions for performing prayers.

ISLAMIC SYMBOLS

The Islamic year follows the lunar calendar. Consequently many take the crescent as a symbol of Islam as such, so much more so since the Red Crescent organization is the Muslim equivalent to the Red Cross. In fact, several Muslim countries display a green or red crescent in their national flags (Algeria, the Maldives, Mauretania, Pakistan, Turkey).

Nevertheless, the crescent originally was not associated with Islam; it rather is a popularized Turkish symbol. Nor was the green color—now used for the turbans worn by descendants of the prophet—originally Islamic. The first Muslim flags were in fact black. Nevertheless, not only the Muslims but the entire world by now associate both green and the crescent with Islam.

PROSPECTS

The 21st century has already seen much strife with religious colors.

Even so, the world religions in the course of their tragically violent histories have never been as close to each other as today, in the age of the digital revolution.

As a cynic one might attribute this mood for conciliation to the observation that "absolute truth becomes tolerant only when it is no longer fully believed" (Josef van Esch, S.J.). But religious tolerance should not be the result of a destructive relativism. Rather it should result from a "global theology" (Wilfred Cantwell Smith). Such a theology must insist on the fundamental difference between the common search for the ultimate transcendental Reality and its various symbolic expressions.

This is the theology which has made possible the rise of a world oecumenical movement, characterized by a more sociological than mystical concept of faith.

Muslims welcome this development in as much as it allows them to participate. Instead of the previous danger of *exclusivism* they now sense a new danger in form of an all-embracing *inclusivism* that might rob them of their identity.

As it is, there is a visible chance that at least the three monotheistic religions will return to their common Ibrahimic roots whose essence is the peace giving submission to God: Islam in its profound original sense.

After the rationalistic 18th century, the atheistic 19th century and the ideological 20th century, in the 21st century the world promises a return to religion. New physics (Quantum Mechanics and Relativity Theories) via its de-materialization leads straight back to the notion of God.

Already the sociology of religion admits that its prediction of a gradual demise of religion had been wrong to an embarrassing degree.

While formerly it had been undisputed that religion will disappear to the degree science increases, recent champions of the Tao of Physics (Fritjof Capra) realize that both science and religion can grow simultaneously. This is indeed the case now. Muslims now also profit from the recognition that they do not only pursue their claims (want things) but have something precious to offer (give things): their value conservatism which is resistant to moral or immoral fashions. In this perspective Islam contributes to a cultural revolution on whose outcome the survival of the Western civilization may well depend.

CHRONOLOGY

569/570	Birth of the Prophet Muhammad in Mecca.
610	Beginning of the Qur'anic revelation.
621	Muhammad`s mystical night journey to Jerusalem and Heaven.
622	Flight to al-Madinah.
	Founding of a Muslim-Jewish Confederation.
628	Muhammad`s messages to other rulers.
630	Peaceful conquest of Mecca.
632	Farewell Pilgrimage; Muhammad dies.
632-34	Abu Bakr (1st) Caliph; Qur'an collection consolidated.
634-44	'Umar ibn al-Khattab (2nd) Caliph.
	Iraq, Syria, Jordan, Palestine become Muslim.
644-56	'Uthman ibn 'Affan (3rd) Caliph.
	Qur'an copied and distributed.
	Egypt and Persia Muslim.
656-61	'Ali ibn Abi Talib (4th and last "rightly guided).
	Caliph. Zypres and Afghanistan Muslim.
661	Battle of Siffin. Muslims split into Sunnis, Shi'ites and Kharijis (Secessionists).
656-750	Umayyad dynasty in Damascus.
711	Andalusia Muslim.
712	India`s west coast Muslim.
713	Turkmenistan Muslim.
732	Muslim invasion into central France.
750-1258	Abbasid dynasty in Baghdad.
786-809	Harun al-Rashid.
	Collection of the Traditions of the Prophet.
	Creation of the Islamic Schools of Law.
	First blooming of Muslim mysticism (Sufism).
	Development of Islamic philosophy.

756-1031	Umayyad (counter-) caliphate in Cordoba, followed by North African Berber reform movements in Andalusia (al-Murabitun / al-Muwahidun).
909-1171	Fatimide (counter-) caliphate in Cairo.
980-1937	Avicenna (Ibn Sina).
1058-1111	Abu Hamid al-Ghasali (al-Gazel).
1096-1291	(Five) Crusades.
1099	Sack of Jerusalem.
1126-1198	Averroës (Ibn Rushd).
1165-1240	Muhy ad-Din ibn al-'Arabi.
1187	Saladin (Salah ad-Din) retakes Jerusalem.
1207-73	Jalal ad-Din Rumi.
1258	Mongols conquer Baghdad and kill last Abbaside caliph.
1263-1328	Ibn Taymiyyah.
1280-1918	Ottoman Empire. Anatolia Muslim.
1322-1406	Ibn Khaldun.
1389	Ottoman victory over the Serbs at Kosovo Polje.
1453	Ottomans occupy Constantinople (Istanbul).
1458	Bosnia Muslim.
1492	Fall of Granada; Muslim rule in Andalusia ends.
1516	Muslims and Jews exiled from Spain. Inquisition.
1518	Sultan Selim I first Ottoman caliph.
1529	Ottoman siege of Vienna.
1563-1624	Ahmad al-Sirhindi.
1571	Sea battle of Lepanto.
1578	Battle of the Three Kings at Ksar el-kebir (Morocco). End of Portuguese invasion into North Africa.
1683	Second (and last) Ottoman siege of Vienna.
18th cent.	Religious renewal begins (Shah Wali Allah; Muhammad ibn 'Abd al-Wahhab).
1798	Napoleon I in Egypt. Colonization begins.
1839-97	Al-Afghani creates pan-Islamic world movement.

1849-1904	Muhammad Abduh. Beginning of Salafiyyah reforms.
1857	Britain destroys Moghul rule in India.
1873-1960	Said Nursi, religious opponent of Mustafa Kemal in Turkey.
1873-1938	Muhammad Iqbal, spiritual father of Pakistan.
1900-92	Muhammad Asad alias Leopold Weiss.
1906-66	Sayyid Qutb.
1924	Caliphate abolished in Turkey.
1928	Foundation of the Muslim Brothers by Hassan al-Banna.
1932	Saudi Arabia becomes Kingdom.
1941	Foundation of Jama´at-al Islami by Abu-l-´Ala al-Mawdudi.
1947	Creation of Pakistan as an Islamic State.
1965	Publication of Sayyid Qutb`s book "Milestones"; Qutb executed.
1945-62	Decolonization of Muslim countries completed.
1970-90	Mass emigration of Muslims to Western Europe and North America.
2001	Attack against World Trade Center in New York and Pentagon in Washington, D.C. ("9/11").
2002– ...	War on Terror against ´Usama bin Laden`s al-Qa`ida.

Selective Literature

General Literature

Aldamer, Shafi, *Saudi Arabia and Britain*, Reading 2003

Armstrong, Karen, *Holy War–The Crusades and their Impact on Today's World*, New York 1992

Asad, Muhammad, *The Road to Mecca*, New York 1954

Banna, Hassan al-, *Five Tracts*, Berkeley 1975

Bennis, Phyllis, *Before and After–US Foreign Policy and the War on Terrorism*, Gloustershire (UK) 2003

Bukhari, al-, *Sahih al-Bukhari*, 9 vol., Chicago 1976-79

Chapra, Umer *The Future of Economics*, Markfield (UK) 2000

Daniel, Norman, *Islam and the West–The Making of an Image*, Oxford 2nd ed. 1993

Davidson, Lawrence, *Islamic Fundamentalism*, Westport, Connecticut, 1998

Esposito, John, *Voices of Resurgent Islam*, Oxford 1983

Ghazali, Abu Hamid al-, *Ihya Ulum-id Din*, 4 vol., Lahore (n.d.)

Guillaume, A., *The Life of Muhammad*, Oxford 1955

Hamidullah, Muhammad, *The Emergence of Islam*, Islamabad 1993

Hofmann, Murad, *Religion on the Rise–Islam in the Third Millennium*, Beltsville, MD 2001

Izetbegovic, 'Alija, *Islam between West and East*, Indianapolis, 2nd ed. 1989

Ibn Khaldun, *The Muqaddima, An Introduction to History*, Princeton 1967

Iqbal, Muhammad, *The Reconstruction of Religious Thought*, Lahore (many editions)

Jayyusi, Salma Khadra (ed.), *The Legacy of Muslim Spain*, Leyden 1992

Lawrence, Bruce, *Shattering the Myth–Islam beyond Violence*, Princeton 1998

Malik b. Anas, *Al-Muwatta*, Norwich 1982

Motzki, Harald, *The Origins of Islamic Jurisprudence*, Leyden 2002

Nasr, Seyyed Hossein, *Ideal and Realities of Islam*, Cairo 1989

Napoleoni, Loretta, *Modern Jihad*, London 2003

Osman, Fathi, *Concepts of the Qur'an*, Los Angeles 1997

Qutb, Sayyid, *Milestones*, Indianapolis 1990

Rahman, Fazlur, *Islam*, New York 1966

Robinson, Neal, *Discovering the Qur'an*, London 1996

Said, Edward, *Orientalism*, New York 1978

Sharif, M.M. (ed.), *A History of Islamic Philosophy*, 2 vol., Wiesbaden 1963-66

Turabi, Hassan al-, *Islam, Democracy, the State and the West*, Tampa, Florida 1993

Wolfe, Michael, *One Thousand Roads to Mecca*, New York 1997

Woodward, Bob, *Plan of Attack*, New York 2004

CONTACTS

I. IN GREAT BRITAIN

Association of Muslim Social Scientists (AMSS / UK)
P. O. Box 126
Richmond, Surrey TW9 2LS
Tel. + 1-208-948.9511

Forum against Islamophobia and Racism (FAIR)
Suite 19, Jubilee Business Centre, Exeter Road
London NW2 3UF
Tel. +44-207-8453.7501

Centre for Islamic Studies
("Journal of Qur'anic Studies")
School of Oriental and African Studies
London University
Thornhaughe Street, Russel Square
London WC1H OXG
Tel. + 44-181-886.9952

International Forum for Islamic Dialogue (IFID)
BM Box 5826
London WC1 N3XX
+ 44-208-903.8958

The Islamic Foundation /
Markfield Institute of Higher Education (MIHE)
("Encounters"; "The Muslim World Book Review")
Ratby Lane
Markfield, Leicestershire LE67 9SY
Tel. + 44-1530-244.944

al-Khoei Foundation
Stone Hall, Chevening Road
London NW6 6TN
Tel. + 44-171-372.4049

Muslim Association of Britain (MBA)
233, Seven Sisters Road
London N4 2DA
Tel. +44-207-272.2888

Oxford Centre for Islamic Studies (OCIS)
"Oxford Journal for Islamic Studies"
George Street
Oxford OX1 2AR
Tel. + 1-865-278.730

II. IN THE UNITED STAATES

American Muslim Council (AMC)
Suite 400, 1212 New York Ave., N.W.
Washington, D.C., 2005-6102
Tel. + 1 - 202 - 789.2262

Association of Muslim Social Scientists (AMSS / US)
P. O. Box 699
Herndon, VA 20172
+ 1 - 703-471.1133

Center for Muslim-Christian Understanding
Georgetown University
37th & O Streets, N.W.
Washington, D.C. 20057
Tel. + 1 - 202 - 687.8575

Center for the Study of Islam and Democracy
P. O. Box 864
Burtonville, MD 20866
Tel. + 1 - 202 - 251.30865

Council for American-Islamic Relations (CAIR)
453 New Jersey Avenue, SE
Washington, D.C. 2003
Tel. + 1 - 202 - 488.8787

International Institute of Islamic Thought (IIIT)
("American Journal of Islamic Social Studies")
P. O. Box 699 / 555, Grove Street
Herndon, VA 22070-4705

Islamic Council of North America (ICNA)
166-26, 89th Ave.
Jamaica, N. Y. 11432
Tel. + 1 -718- 658.1199

Islamic Legal Studies Program
Pound Hall 501
Harvard Law School HFB 314
Cambridge, MA 02138
Tel. + 1 - 617-496.3941

Islamic Society of North America (ISNA)
("Horizons")
6555, South Country Road
Plainfield, IN 46168
Tel. + 1 - 317-839.8157

United Association for Studies and Research
("Middle East Affairs Journal")
P. O. Box 1210
Annandale, VA 22003
Tel. + 1 - 703-750.9011

– Part Two –

An Introduction to The Qur'an

INTRODUCTION

The Qur'an is a Universe that speaks.
The Universe is a silent Qur'an.

– Arab Wisdom

To have accepted writing about the Qur'an seems pretty frivolous to me now.

Someone who introduces a subject, does he not pretend to master it? But that in case of the Qur'an is out of anybody's reach.

Say: "If the seas were ink for the words of my Lord, indeed the ink would be exhausted before the words of my Lord came to an end, even if We added the same amount (of ink) again"
(18: 109; similarly 31: 27).

In fact, nobody's erudition and life span could possibly do half-way justice to this scripture. Even prolonged cooperation between an expert team in the Arab language, theology, philosophy, history, anthropology, psychology, sociology, literature, physics, and biology would never arrive at final conclusions, because the Qur'an keeps offering new insights to every individual, every society, in each new era. In other words: Never ever is the Qur'an without relevance.

So it figures that Paul Schwarzenau, a Protestant theologian, experienced the Qur'an as "an enormous, endlessly faceted jewel, illuminated from within and radiating in all directions". He found that each of its segments reflects archetypical images. Schwarzenau had indeed come to understand the Qur'an not as God's *incarnation* (becoming man) but as His *inlibrettion* (becoming a text).

However, not everyone finds easy access to this book. Some are even disaffected by what they see as disorder and abrupt thematic changes–poetic images, moral appeals, narratives, and down-to-earth instructions appearing side by side. How to cope with a text which is repetitive and constantly shifting not only from one subject matter to the next but also from one grammatical person (: I, We, He) and one grammatical tense (: past, present, future) to the other?

No wonder that the Qur'an at times provokes emotional rejection. The great German poet and thinker Johann Wolfgang von Goethe, for instance, found himself both attracted and repulsed by this book. In his *West-Eastern Divan* he wrote that this is a book which "every time we approach it disgusts us anew but then fascinates us, astonishes us and, in the end, compels our admiration".

One cannot discuss the Qur'an without knowing something about Muhammad. Neither can one discuss the Qur'an nor Muhammad without touching Islam. This was done in Part 1 of this book.

Of course, I do not attempt to make reading the Qur'an itself superfluous. On the contrary, while going through this book the Qur'an should constantly be at hand.

EDITORIAL NOTE

1. In Western languages the word "Qur'an" mostly is spelled "Koran". This does, however, double injustice to the pronunciation of this Arab word because in Arabic "q" and "k" sound differently; also, as indicated by the apostrophe its two syllables are pronounced separately.

2. One refers to verses of the Qur'an by listing surah and verse numbers, separated by colon. Thus "2: 185" indicates verse 185 of the 2nd Surah. In comparison, the numbers of chapters and verses of the Bible are separated by comma.

3. The Arab name for the one and only divinity, Allah, is given here as "God" in order to underline that Muslims do not have a divinity separate from the Christian or Jewish one. However, it must be kept in mind that the Muslim *image* of God is free of Christian associations like Incarnation and Trinity.

4. Whenever Muslims pronounce the names of prophets like Jesus or Muhammad they add the benediction "[God`s] peace be upon him!" In books mainly addressed to Muslims this is indicated by adding in each case "pbuh" or "s." for *sallalahu 'alaihi wa-s-salam.*

The Qur'an as Holy Script

God is the One Who does not appear in His appearances.
— Martin Buber

Myths, sagas, legends, oracles, popular wisdom, religious hymns and magic formulas are the memory of mankind. Some of it has been written down.

And a few of these scripts are considered holy.

In Hindu heritage this is the case with the Vedas ("Knowledge"), including their commentary (Shrooti), the Upanishads, the 36 volume Puranas ("The Preceding"), as well as the Mahabharata epic and the religious poem Bhagawad Gita. They probably date from 1200 to 1000 before the Common Era (CE).

The Buddhist world as well possesses holy scriptures. They include the Pali-Canon with its three "baskets" (Tripitaka) and the Sanskrit-Canon as well as scripts like Lalitavistara, Mahavastu, Saddharmapundarika and Prajnaparamita. Their focus is a historical personality: Siddharth Gautama (560-480 BCE). But their authors cannot be determined with any certainty; some of these scriptures only surfaced after Christ.

The Mosaic religion is based on the Bible (Old Testament), holy script *par excellence*. Yet the Hebrew Bible is a collection of writings of very different age, covering 1800 years of development and combining different traditional strands. As a rule, the true authors of the various books of the Bible are unknown. What is accepted as "Bible" by Jews, Orthodox Christians, Catholics and Protestants, respectively, is not identical. Rather, Jews and the various Christian churches use Bibles of different composition. This explains why Catholics until 1965 were forbidden to read any but their own Biblical version.

For most Christians the New Testament, dealing with the life and teachings of Jesus, is the key text. It consists of 27 scripts, including the four canonical Evangels and the letters by St Paul, written by a number of authors between the years 50 and 130 after Christ. The present composition of the New Testament is the result of a drawn-out sifting process lasting into the second half of the 4th century.

None of the components of the New Testament are written in Jesus` own language, Aramaic, but rather in Hebrew and Greek. This is the dilemma behind the rather speculative postulate that there must have been a collection of Jesus` sayings (Logia Jesu), now lost: a mysterious source called "Q" (from the German word for source, Quelle). Today, Christian historical critique of the New Testament is unanimous in its conclusion that the four Evangels, the Apocalypse and the so-called Catholic Letters have not been written by the people whose names they bear. They are also agreed that none of these parts of the New Testament have been written by a disciple of Jesus. In fact, the oldest and the only fully authentic part of the New Testament are the Letters by St. Paul; but he never met, or spoke with, Jesus. (Needless to say that Muslims reject all documents which cannot be attributed to, or are severed from, their sources.)

Against this background one will immediately appreciate the Qur'an as the only truly authentic holy script, indeed as a sacred source *sui generis*, being the only one of its kind. This is due to the fact the Qur'an

- originated in the 7th century CE, i.e. in the full light of documented history;
- was immediately committed to writing;
- had one author only, Muhammad b.´Abdallah, whose life is known in all detail;
- exists in the very language in which it was communicated;
- has been preserved immaculately.

THE QUR'AN AS REVELATION

The qualification "holy" is attributed to scriptures whose message is seen as true beyond question, whose origin is considered supra-natural, and whose awe inspiring authority is undisputably binding. In this sense now only the Qur'an qualifies. The Muslim community (ummah) is the only religious group which still sees its foundational document as a divine *verbal revelation*: Sentence for sentence, nay, word for word sent down (nazala) by Him, representing His very speech (kalam Allah).

Except for a small minority of Jewish and Christian fundamentalists, all other so-called holy texts are no longer considered verbal revelations but, at best, as *inspired* wisdom. Yet inspiration (al-ilham) is categorically different from revelation. An inspired person, like the young Albert Einstein, all of a sudden and without knowing how, may hit upon a sensationally workable idea. In contrast, revelation reveals God as its source.

For Muslims acknowledging the genuineness of the Qur'anic revelation is indispensible. Someone unconvinced of it simply is not a Muslim. To reserve the qualification "fundamentalist" for *politically active* Muslims is therefore misleading. In as much as fundamentalism refers to believing in scriptural inerrancy, *all* Muslims by definition are fundamentalists.

The Formation of the Qur'an

At the same time, the Qur'an is the last book of antiquity and the first modern book.

— Paul Schwarzenau

How revelation began

At the end of the month of Ramadan in 610 CE, as usual from time to time Muhammad, just 40, had withdrawn for meditation to the loneliness of Jabal an-Nur (Mountain of Light), five kilometers to the north-east of Mecca. There in a cave called Hira, he used to ponder and pray. While slumbering he was overcome by the vision that an angel–Gabriel–repeatedly ordered him to read. Each time Muhammad alleged his illiteracy as excuse. Upon which the angel spoke:

> **Recite in the name of your Lord Who created–**
> **Created man from something that clings!**
> **Recite ! For your Lord is merciful,**
> **He Who taught with the help of the pen–**
> **Taught Man what he did not know.** (96: 1-5)

That Night of Fate (lailat al-qadr), on 25, 27 or 29 Ramadan, the Qur'anic revelation began. It is the foundational miracle of Islam.

Deeply shaken Muhammad returned to his wife, Khadija, asking her to cover him. Having regained his composure he started wondering whether he was right in his mind. That he might have been chosen as receptacle of supra-natural messages was entirely inconceivable for him.

Doubts about himself became sheer unbearable when Muhammad for the next three years received no further communications from beyond (fatra al-wahy). But then he heard Gabriel say:

> **Truly, We shall entrust you with a weighty word.** (73: 5)

And: **You are favored by your Lord and not possessed.** (68: 2)

And: **Oh you, covered one, rise and warn, and glorify your Lord.** (74: 1-3)

And: **Your Lord did not desert you, and you are not displeasing Him...And your Lord will soon convey to you, and you shall be content. Did He not find you as an orphan and take you in? And did He not find you lost and guided you?** (93: 3, 5-7)

Subsequently, altogether for 23 years, Muhammad received further divine communications, until shortly before his death in 632 CE. In the process, he became both prophet and statesman, and the communications received by him had taken shape as a book: the Qur'an ("what is to be recited").

Revelations reached the Prophet in different ways - while awake and while sleeping, even on horseback. Only twice Gabriel appeared to him directly, luminously. Muhammad himself described the process of revelation as follows: "Sometimes it reaches me like the chiming of church bells. This is the toughest way for me. When it ceases, I recall what had been told."

Apparently during the revelation of "weighty a word" Muhammad turned into an instrument. His wife 'A`isha observed that during revelations he would start sweating, even on cold days.

In 621 CE Muhammad as a *real vision* experienced travelling to Jerusalem (al-miraj), followed by his Nightly Journey to heaven (al-isra`). This over-whelming revelatory experience is powerfully reflected in the Qur'an (17: 1, 60; 53: 1-18). During it the Prophet was "out of himself", yet intellectually alert, deeply stirred, yet observant:

By the star when it sinks !
Your companion does not err, nor is he deceived.
Nor does he speak of his own desire.
It [the Qur'an] is nothing but a revealed revelation
which the one mighty in power taught him, the wise one.
He stood there, clear to view, on the uppermost horizon.

Then he drew near and came close
till he was at a distance of two bows` length or even nearer.
And he revealed to his servant what he had to reveal.
The heart did not lie in seeing what it saw.
Will you then dispute with him what he saw ?
Verily, he saw him yet another time
By the lote-tree of the utmost boundary
near the garden of abode
when the lote-tree was shrouded by what shrouded it.
The eye did not turn aside, nor was it overbold.
Verily, he saw one of the greatest signs of his Lord. (53: 1-18)

The Qur'an itself and the Prophet`s narratives demonstrate that

- Muhammad was totally surprised when revelation reached him. He had not planned for himself a prophetic career;
- the revelatory act was not associated with symptoms of pathological disturbances like epileptic seizures or schizophrenia;
- revelation in most cases reached Muhammad not visually but orally; typologically Muhammad was an auditive prophet;
- being illiterate Muhammad was unable to draw on existing religious scripts;
- Muhammad had never made a name for himself as a poet (ash sha`ir) or seer (al-kahin).

What had happened to him is described in the Qur'an as follows:

It is not given to any human being that God should speak to him except by inspiration (al-wahy) or from behind a veil or by sending a messenger to reveal what He wills by His leave...And thus We have sent to you of the spirit of Our command. You did not know what the scripture was nor what was faith. But We made a light with which We guide whom of Our servants We will. And you are indeed guiding on to a straight path. (43: 51-53)

These verses amount to a theory of prophethood.

WHO WAS MUHAMMAD ?

Muhammad's life after the beginning of revelation is recorded in amazing detail since, from then on, he had become a historical personality of the first order. The same is not true for the preceding two-thirds of his life during which he had failed to draw attention to himself in public. Muhammad belonged to the Hashimite clan of the south-Arabic tribe of Qura'ish, living in Mecca. Ever since 'Abd al-Muttalib, one of his ancestors, Muhammad's family was in charge of feeding pilgrims and providing them with water from the fountain of Zamzam, located in the vicinity of the town's famous temple, the Ka'aba.

Born after the death of his father 'Abdullah, in 569 or 570 CE, Muhammad as a four-year-old boy was entrusted to the Banu Sa'ad, a bedouin tribe, where his foster mother Halima was to teach him the values and ways of the desert Arab. He lost his mother, Amina, when only six years of age and his remaining grandfather at eight.

From then on, Muhammad, the orphan, was taken care of by his influential uncle Abu Talib, father of his cousin 'Ali. Abu Talib took Muhammad along on caravan tours, all the way to Syria, and turned him into an accomplished trader. In this capacity Muhammad found many a chance to excel morally. For being sincere, honest and reliable to an unusual degree people began calling him the Trustworthy (al-Amin). This explains why Meccans called on him when the Ka'aba, destroyed by a flood of rain, had to be rebuilt in 594 CE.

The different clans of Mecca, extremely honor-conscious and jealous of each other, could only agree on Muhammad for the prestigious task of restoring the Black Stone (al-hajar al-aswad) to its original place in a corner of the temple walls. Muhammad's family had become so poor that he could hardly even think of getting married. However, in 595 CE Khadija, owner of a well-to-do export / import firm, asked *him* into marriage (not the other way around). She had been widowed twice and was 15 years his elder. For 25 years, until her death in 619, Khadija and Muhammad as partners both in marriage and business led an extraordinarily happy family life. They had six children of whom Fatima, later wife of 'Ali, became mother of *all* of the Prophet`s descendants. (Her siblings had all died in childhood.)

Khadija was the first person (and thus Muslim) to believe in Muhammad`s prophetic mission, before being joined by Abu Bakr, his best friend, and his cousin 'Ali. At first, this tiny circle of Muslims only increased slowly, mainly among underprivileged people like Bilal, a black slave who later became the first caller to prayer (al muadhdhin) in Islam.

This small original community of Muslims met clandestinely in a private home–al-Arkam–near today`s Great Mosque. But from 613 Muhammad began preaching in public. Gradually, Islam developed into a religion whose teachings challenged all other faiths:

- There is only one God, both immanent and transcendent. (This doctrine called *al-tawhid* is the essence of Islam.)
- God is benevolent. (For Arabs a strange idea.)
- God has neither daughters nor sons.
- There exist non-visible, spiritual creatures of God (angels; jins).
- There is life after death, both in heaven (al-jannah) or hell (al- jahannam). (For Arabs another strange idea.)
- Peoples` fate in the other world depends on their behavior in this world. (Arabs rather felt subject to fate.)
- Nobody is responsible for somebody else`s actions. (Arabs practiced collective guilt, as in blood revenge.)
- Man`s purpose in life is to recognize God and praise Him.
- Muhammad, like all prophets including Jesus, is human only.
- He restored the original, pristine monotheism of Abraham, diluted by both Christianity (: Trinity) and Judaism (: Chosen People).

These points, most of them of theological nature, made up the core messages of the *Meccan* Qur'an. These were later completed in al-Madinah with a more detailed rejection of Jewish notions (Chosen People; Covenant between God and Man) and Christian ones (Hereditary Sin; Incarnation; Trinity; priesthood; celibacy). Both during the Meccan and Medinan periods of revelation the Qur'an also dealt with questions of ritual, ethics, and community life (family law; inheritance; economics; penal law).

The Meccan families had been exposed to Jews and Christians without ever feeling threatened by their teachings or style of life. In the case of Islam the situation was different. Muhammad and his followers increasingly had to endure insult, abuse, and even violence directed against the most vulnerable among them. Muhammad found himself accused of being a liar, imposter, social revolutionary, and blasphemer, dangerously insulting the city's protective goddesses al-Lat, al-'Uzza and Manat. In short, Muhammad was blamed for disturbing local peace and upsetting Meccan prosperity which depended on the tolerant polytheistic cult of the Ka'aba. By risking to disturb the heathen pilgrimage to Mecca, the Prophet was indeed a threat for the Meccan establishment.

As reflected in the 111th Surah, the protagonists of the leading Umayyad clan, including Abu Sufyan, Abu Jahl and Abu Lahab, were particularly hostile to the Muslim community. When their persecution reached its zenith, Muhammad in 615 CE advised the majority of his followers to seek asylum with the Christian ruler of Abyssinia. In fact 107 Muslims, of whom 18 were women, temporarily emigrated. Their expectations of finding religious tolerance were met by the Negus.

As long as the early Muslims remained in Mecca, the Prophet did not allow self-defense against the vicious treatment meted out to them. Patience and forbearance, not resistance, was the order. He himself had to endure a policy alternating between flattery (offering him kingship) and punishment (economic boycott from 616-619). However, after both his wife Khadija and his protector Abu Talib had died in 619 and the Meccans even had tried to assassinate him, Muhammad, too, had to leave town.

In 620, together with Abu Bakr, his friend and father-in-law, Muhammad clandestinely made his way to the conglomeration of Yathrib, 400 km north of Mecca, which already had a sizeable community of local Muslims. In 621 and again in 622, at Aqaba, 72 of them had invited their Meccan brothers in faith to move to Yathrib and settle among them. When most of the Meccan Muslims (and those in Abyssinia as well) took up that offer they became "migrants" (al-muhajirun) and 622 CE the "year of migration" (al-hijra) with which the Islamic calendar begins. (Currently we are in 1428 a.h. / anno hijri.)

From now on Yathrib became the "City of the Prophet" (al-Madinah an-Nabi) shortened to "al-Madinah". Here the Prophet created specific bonds of friendship between each family of the migrants and a family of their Madinan "helpers" (an-ansar). Equally important, on the basis of a constitution dictated by him he created a confederation between the Arab Muslim tribes and the Jewish ones in al-Madinah. Thus he became a head of State, and the Qur'an now started to demand obedience to "God and His Prophet" (e.g. in 8: 46; 47: 33).

The expectation that the Jewish tribes of al-Madinah either would accept Islam or as a minimum remain neutral in its armed conflict with Mecca did not come true. The Jews collaborated with Mecca against the Muslim communities of al-Madinah and revolted against them, provoking their own expulsion.

Shortly after arriving in al-Madinah Muhammad married 'A'isha, daughter of his best friend Abu Bakr. A number of other weddings, mostly dynastic in nature, followed, designed to stabilize strategically important friendships and the State.

Mecca viewed the developments in al-Madinah with alarm, feeling that its ideological and economic leadership in all of Arabia was at stake. They decided to seek a military solution. Now Al-Madinah for years had to defend itself against repeated Meccan campaigns. In accordance with the Qur'an Muhammad now allowed armed resistance.

The first clash, in the month of Ramadan in 624, occurred near Badr, half way between al-Madinah and the Red Sea. In spite of their numerical inferiority–324 Muslims against 950 Meccans–the Muslims won in dramatic fashion.

This skirmish was followed by two full fledged sieges of al-Madinah: The uneven stand-off near the mountain of Uhud, in 625, where 700 Muslims fought 3000 Meccans and Muhammad was wounded; and the battle of the Ditch (al-khandaq), in 727, when 1500 Muslims stood their ground against, and demoralized, 10.000 Meccan warriors.

The balance of power now favored al-Madinah. So Muhammad could dare, in 628, to lead 1400 Muslim pilgrims towards Mecca, for Umrah (little pilgrimage). This was a brilliant move, causing panic in Mecca and leading, in near-by Hudaybiyya, to an armistice, postponing the pilgrimage to the following year, thus anticipating the capitulation of Mecca. In 630, after eight years of absence, Muhammad himself was able to return to his home city, victorious and accompanied by no less than 10.000 Muslims. As if by silent plebiscite, the entire city, including its titular leader, Abu Sufyan, had become Muslim.

Now, purged of its 360 idols, the Ka'aba became again the very temple of monotheism it had been at the time of Abraham. Now, Mecca became the "qibla", i.e. the direction in which Muslims offer their prayer.

Even before, in 628, the Prophet had begun to globalize Islam by inviting all rulers in his vicinity to accept Islam. Such letters went to Heraclius, Byzantine emperor in Constantinople, to Shah Khosrau II, the Persian emperor, and to Maukakis, the Coptic archbishop of Alexandria. The latter letter, written on leather, is on display in the Topkapi Museum in Istanbul.

In 632, three months before his death, Muhammad performed his only great pilgrimage (al-hajj) according to the new Islamic rite. This event, now called Farewell Pilgrimage, was already attended by an incredible 140.000 Muslim pilgrims. On that occasion, from mount 'Arafat, Muhammad delivered a touching sermon in which he urged

the Muslims to do justice to their wives and verified with them that
he had transmitted his divine message, fully and unabridged. In one
of the very last revelations the Prophet was assured of being the last
prophet ever, i.e. the seal (al-khatam) of prophethood, and that Islam
is the religion ordained by God (5: 5).

On 8 June, 632, Muhammad died in the arms of his wife 'A`isha
and was buried in her room. His abode, including its garden
(ar-rawda), forms part of the Prophet`s Mosque in al-Madinah which
now provides space for no less than 480.000 people praying.

MUHAMMAD IN THE QUR'AN

Muhammad is not the author of the Qur'an but its transmitter.
Also this book does not have him but the Qur'an as its subject.

If one knows his life well one can find clues for it in the Qur'an.
But his life could not possibly be reconstructed from the Qur'anic
text.

Of personalities in his vicinity only two are mentioned in the
Qur'an: Abu Lahab and Zayd; of historical Islamic places only Mecca
(Bakka), Yathrib (al-Madinah), 'Arafat, Badr, al-Hijr, and Hunayn.

The 47th Surah has been named "Muhammad". But his name
appears only four times in the entire Qur'an. However, in the Qur'an
God frequently addresses Himself directly to him, frequently with the
order "Say: ... "(qul...), calling him His messenger and warner.

Most importantly the Qur'an makes clear that Muhammad is

- merely a human being who eats and drinks and "goes to the
  market";
- no poet (sha`ir) and no sooth-sayer (al-kahin);
- the last prophet ever (33: 40);
- without power to work miracles;
- only charged to deliver, not to impose, God`s message.

It is not always flattering for the Prophet when he is mentioned
in the Qur'an.

On the contrary, repeatedly God reprimanded him severely. In

66: 1 he is reproached: **Why do you forbid what God has allowed?** In 18: 23 f. he is blamed for having envisaged a new, explicatory revelation on the following day instead of leaving that in God`s discretion. The 80th Surah contains the most severe reprimand because Muhammad had frowned when a poor blind man had interrupted his conversation with an influential personality:

He frowned and turned away because the blind man
came to him.
How would you know that he did not want to become pure
Or seek and profit from your admonition?
As for him who thinks himself self-sufficient
to him you pay attention......
But as to him who eagerly comes to you,
fearful of God,
him you neglect.
Not so! This is an admonishment!

A fourth passage critical of the Prophet (13: 37) will be discussed in connection with the so-called Satanic Verses.

All this is remarkable in view of the fact that critique of Prophets is unknown to all other holy scripts, although they report inadmissible, even immoral behavior as, for instance, by David in the Bible. The fact that the Qur'an is critical of Muhammad may be taken as circumstantial evidence proving that he is not its author.

THE COLLECTION OF THE QUR'AN

THE QUR'AN DURING THE LIFETIME OF THE PROPHET

At the time of the Prophet Muhammad writing was a rare skill, given that the Arabic alphabet had only been invented during his youth, in the al-Anbar region north-west of Baghdad, and that by three men whose names have come down to us: Murmit b. Murwah, Aslam b. Sidrah, and Amir b. Hidrah.

Al-Nadim (d. 995) in his annotated bibliography "al-Fihrist" expresses the considered opinion that the Arabic letters were developed both from the Nabatean script and the Himyarite letter system found in the Yemen. At any rate, at the beginning of Muhammad`s mission reading and writing were not taught in school in Mecca, there was not a single book available, and only 17 Meccans had somehow learned how to read. (100 years later the Muslim nation had become the most literate on a global scale.)

In the absence of written records people of that era performed amazing feats of memorization. Many people were able to recite from memory very long poems, *ghazals* and *qasidas*. It is therefore entirely believable that many Muslims contemporary to the Prophet knew the entire Qur'an by heart. Of course, social control at that time was such that nobody could have added anything to the Qur'anic text.

Every time a new verse "came down" it became talk of the town. After all, many a revelation—like the prohibition of alcohol —immediately impacted on the life of the entire community. Muhammad used to recite new Qur'anic passages first to a gathering of men and next to a gathering of women. Also, he recited new verses in his prayer, in the mosque. Consequently, if someone made a mistake when quoting from the Qur'an, he was immediately corrected.

(This is still the habit today. If an *imam* slips during recitation, his attention will be drawn to it by people injecting "al-hamdulillah!").

The process of collective Qur'an memorization was promoted by the Prophet's practice to recite the entire Qur'an aloud, in the mosque, during the month of Ramadan. During his final year, he did this twice.

In addition, the Prophet took care that the Qur'an would be written down as it developed. Paper was yet unknown. But one could write on wood, leather, palm leaves, stones and bones. Two dozen secretaries of the Prophet (al-katib al-wahy) under Zayd b. Thabit, his chief secretary (katib an-nabi), were charged with recording the revelations. In each case, the Prophet indicated where new texts were to be inserted.

At that time, the Qur'an existed in the form of loose-leaf collections properly described as *al-mushaf* (leaves) but even then already called "the book" (al-kitab). This way of proceeding made it possible for the Prophet in Mecca to provide the Muslims of the Banu Zurayq clan in al-Madinah with a copy of the Qur'an (as then existing).

Aside from complete collections of the Qur'anic text-in-progress there were individual leaves, private recordings of certain Surahs or parts of them. This fact is documented by an event that led to the dramatic conversion of 'Umar b. al-Khattab, later the second Caliph. The text that moved him so–the first eight verses of Surah Ta Ha– he had found with his sister.

STANDARD VERSION OF THE QUR'AN

Full consolidation of the Qur'an was only possible after the Prophet's death because only then the text as it stood was final. At that moment, in addition to many "migrants" (al-muhajirun) there were eight "helpers" (al-ansar) in al-Madinah–all known by name– who had committed the entire Qur'an to memory. One of them, Umm Waraqa, was a woman.

Consolidating the Qur'an into a standard official text soon became urgent because many of the memorizers of the Qur'an (al-huffaz, sing. al-hafiz) lost their lives, be it in battle, be it of old age. Six months after the Prophet's death Abu Bakr, the first Caliph, made a public appeal in al-Madinah commanding each person in possession of a Qur'anic text to come forward and swear that it is identical with what the Prophet had approved.

Zayd b. Thabit, the Prophet's chief secretary, again went into action, this time as editor-in-chief of the consolidated Qur'anic text. He went about this task with utmost care, listening to all those who came forward and comparing their texts with what was already in his possession. His methodology was clear: He would only accept a verse for which, in addition to himself, he found two witnesses. His own memory he only trusted if it was corroborated by others who could assure him of the authenticity of a text.

This first final copy of the Qur'an remained with Caliph Abu Bakr until his death in 644, then with his successor 'Umar until his assassination in 644, and subsequently with his daughter Hafsa, one of the Prophet's wives, who as a *hafiza* knew the Qur'an herself by heart.

During the tenure of 'Uthman, the 3rd Caliph (644-655), the Islamic empire had already spread from North Africa to Afghanistan. Therefore it became a necessity to furnish also remote regions with authentic Qur'anic texts. This moved 'Uthman only 18 years after the Prophet's death to give orders for a copying exercise, this again to be overseen by Zayd b. Thabit. Basis for the exercise was the collection preserved by Hafsa; its outcome was the first book ever written in Arabic. Under Zayd's direction copies were written on parchment (which had become available in the meantime) and forwarded at least to Mecca, Basra, Kufa, and Damascus. One copy was kept by the Caliph himself in al-Madinah. It is now on display in the Topkapi Museum in Istanbul, showing blood stains from 'Uthmans assassination. (Another one of the original copies is again to be found in Tashkent, whereto it was returned from its exile in St. Petersburg.)

In two ways only 'Uthman had interfered in Zayd's historical task: He insisted that in case of conflict preference ought to be given to the pronunciation of Arabic as spoken in Mecca. And he ordered that now, given the availability of an official standard text, all private records of the Qur'an, complete or fragmentary, were to be destroyed.

The latter order was not observed by everyone, if only because pious Muslims could not bring themselves to burning even a snippet that showed part of the Qur'an; they rather "buried" such fragments in sacks, within their mosque. When such material recently was found in the Yemen by Western Orientalists, that was labeled sensational. In the end, however, the Yemeni fragments only confirmed the authenticity of the standard version.

All copies of the Qur'an printed today are authorized copies of authenticated copies from the one prepared by Zayd b. Thabit and his team in the 7th century. They differ only in showing diacritical and vocal marks which were not yet part of the Kufi script used by 7th century calligraphers.

No other religion is in possession of holy scripts whose authenticity is comparable to the one enjoyed by the Qur'an. This is generally recognized by Western Islamologues as well. Rationally no one can dispute the Qur'anic text, its content and provenance from the first half of the 7th century CE.

Open to dispute is, and always will be, only its supra-natural origin since that is not a matter of science but of belief.

MISSING VERSES?
The Shi'ite View

Muslim history has seen serious, at times even violent conflicts between the Sunni majority and the Shi'ite minority. (Currently Shi'i Muslims are mainly found in Iran, 'Iraq, the Lebanon, Bahrain, and the north-eastern part of Saudi Arabia.) In this context, Shi'i Muslims from time to time maintained that certain Qur'anic verses had been suppressed which would have favored 'Ali's claim to the caliphate, as Muhammad's immediate successor. In the 10th century some Shi'ite circles still believed that Fatima, the Prophet's daughter and wife of 'Ali, had been in possession of a different Qur'an, with 17.000 verses three times longer than the standard version.

Such rather wild claims are incompatible with the fact that 'Ali

- participated in a committee supervising 'Uthman's copying exercise;
- as 4th caliph could have seen to it that the Qur'an, if incomplete, was completed.

That he did not interfere shows that he, too, was fully convinced of the completeness of the standard version.

Today, the Shi'i clergy uses the very standard version of the Qur'an that Sunni Muslims use. Their specific views no longer touch the Qur'anic text but find expression only in the way Shi'i commentaries deal with 'Ali and his family.

SATANIC VERSES ?

The question of whether the Qur'an is complete or not came to the fore once more when Salman Rushdie revived the 1400 year old issue of "Satanic Verses". Whether there was such an episode cannot be established because some of the oldest and most reliable sources of Muslim history make no mention of it. This is the case with the famous collections of Prophetic traditions (al-ahadith) by al-Bukhari and by Muslim. Nor is there any trace of "Satanic Verses" in the oldest biography of the Prophet, the one by Ibn Ishaq / Ibn Hisham. However at-Tabari, famous author of a 9th century world history and a very detailed commentary of the Qur'an, relates two incompatible versions of the affair, thus distancing himself from both.

At any rate, some non-Muslims and Muslims as well believe that Muhammad for a while wondered whether he could not overcome the hostility of the Meccan leadership by accepting their goddesses al-Lat, al-'Uzza and Manat, at least as daughters of God (banat Allah), subordinate to Him. It is indeed likely that the Meccan grandees in turn might have honored such a compromise by giving Muhammad a leading position in town.

At this juncture the 53rd Surah had been revealed in whose verses 19 and 20 the question is asked:

Have you then considered al-Lat and al-'Uzza and Manat, the other, third ?

According to a rather doubtful report by Abu al-'Aliya Muhammad was on the point of adding to this text the following "verses" without noticing that they were no revelations but a suggestion by Satan:

"These are the noble (or: high flying) swans (or: cranes) whose assistance is to be hoped for."

News of this development supposedly made the round very quickly, even though the three "goddesses" would have ranked below God, like angels or jinns. It would nevertheless have been sensational for giving legitimacy to the Meccan "goddesses" cult and for accepting the totally un-Islamic idea of intercession thanks to the intervention of intermediate religious figures.

At any rate, the sentence recorded above was never inserted into the Qur'an. Rather Surah 53 in its verses 21-23 continues as follows:

Are the males for you and for Him the females ?
That would be an unfair division.
Verily, these are only names,
named by you and your fathers, without God`s authority.
They only follow a guess and wishful thinking.

With that the three heathen "daughter goddesses" not only had lost their *status*. They were now considered *non-existent*. Islamic monotheism had become even more unequivocal. The Muslims drew a line:

Say: O you disbelievers, I do not worship that which you
worship nor do you worship that which I worship...
To you your religion, and to me my religion (109: 1 f., 6)

From 17: 73 f. can be deduced that Muhammad had been under Meccan pressure to buy their friendship by compromising theologically. Had he not been warned against becoming lenient? The Qur'an in 69: 44-46 could not be more clear-cut:

But if he had attributed to Us a saying invented by him, We surely would have seized him by his right hand and then severed his life artery.

Warned so drastically the Prophet would never have accepted any murky compromise. In fact, he was conscious of the fact that all prophets had to confront the danger of falling victim to Satanic insinuations (22: 52).

If the Satanic Verses episode took place the Qur'anic passages given above can be associated with it. However, these passages do not allow us to conclude *that* the episode had taken place. Nor should one be overly impressed by those early Muslims who had given credence to the episode.

They might indeed have been interested in finding evidence for the disputed thesis that the Qur'anic text includes older verses that were *derogated* by subsequent ones. (This is discussed in the section "Redundant verses?" below.)

Before Salman Rushdie gave prominence to them, the "Satanic Verses"—whether historical or not–were no issue. They still leave Muslims cold because the episode–if it did happen–would only help underline the known fact that Muhammad was totally sincere and entirely human.

LAPIDATION VERSE ?

In the 5th book of Moses, also known as Deuteronomy, the Bible promulgated the death penalty by stoning for adulterers, be they married or not (22, 20-23). The Qur'an equally disapproves of adultery (17: 32) but in 24: 2 replaces capital by corporal punishment (100 lashes). In addition, the Qur'an raises the threshold of necessary evidence to a level that makes it nearly impossible to persecute adultery (4: 15; 24: 4).

It seems that 'Umar ibn al-Khattab, the puritan minded 2nd Caliph, was not entirely happy with this leniency. Repeatedly he mentioned a so-called Verse of Stoning (ayat ar-rajm), dealing with married *adulterers*, that supposedly should have been, but was not, included into the Qur'anic text.

Today, at any rate, Muslims are agreed that no normative text excluded from the Qur'an can be considered Qur'anic.

REDUNDANT VERSES ?

There is a divine promise that the Qur'an will be eternally safeguarded against corruption:

> **Verily We: We it is Who send down the reminder** [the Qur'an] **and surely We will be its Guardian** (15: 9).

Nevertheless, even some of the earliest Muslims disputed that Abu Bakr's loose-leaf Qur'anic collection (al-mushaf) preserved each and every verse ever revealed to Muhammad. In particular, 'Umar held the opinion that a large corpus of earlier revelations had been derogated by later ones and therefore excluded from the written text of the Qur'an. This view is based on 87: 6 f. which says:

> **We shall make you recite so you will not forget except what God wills.**

Like many others, 'Umar may have been misled as well by not always clearly distinguishing between inspired sayings of the Prophet, part of his Sunnah, and revealed texts, part of the Qur'an.

'Umar's theory of derogation is still alive. All commentators of the Qur'an grappled with this issue, and still do: Are there *normative* Qur'anic verses (not *descriptive* ones) which have been superseded by others? If so: Which verses are derogating (an-nasikh) and which ones are derogated (al-mansukh)? To be sure, even derogated verses would formally remain part of the Qur'an and continue to be recited.

Derogation theory owes its existence to the fact that the Qur'an contains verses that *appear* to be mutually exclusive. To be sure, *ontological* truths are not subject to change; theological information (al-akhbar) does not develop. On the other hand, it is indeed conceivable that *normative*, ethical rules (al-ahkam) develop as mankind progresses from rather primitive to more complicated levels of civilization. From this perspective one can see Jewish, Christian, and Islamic law as steady legal refinement, a notion that finds support not only in 16: 101 but above all in 2: 106:

**Whatever verse We abrogate or cause to be forgotten
We bring a better one or one similar to it.**

Many present the "development" of the Qur'anic rules about alcohol as a prime example of derogation:

- First, in 16: 67 the Qur'an mentions alcoholic drinks without passing judgement on it.
- Next, in 2: 219 the Qur'an deals with alcohol as ambivalent, being of some use but mainly evil.
- Then, in 4: 43 the Qur'an disapproves of praying under the influence.
- Finally, in 5: 90 the Qur'an prohibits the consumption of alcohol altogether.

This example illustrates that the concept of derogation can only be handled if one knows the sequence of revelation. Alas, for many individual verses this is not possible.

The example given also illustrates that what superficially looks like a case of derogation may in fact be verses in harmony: Alcohol is indeed ambivalent, useful in medicine for instance; one should not drink it; he who does should at least stay away from prayer. Thus all Qur'anic verses dealing with alcohol are in accord. This is but one of many cases where Qur'an commentators mistook *elaboration* for contradiction.

Derogation theory suffers most, however, from the inability of its supporters to identify clear cases of it. In the Middle Ages, al-Farisi saw 248 cases of derogation, Shah Wali Allah in the 18th century found only five, and the rationalist 9th century Mu'tazila School identified –none.

The latter view is now prevalent. Muhammad Asad when commenting on 2: 106 defeated the very notion of intra-Qur'anic derogation:

- To insinuate that God within a few years needed to correct His norms amounts to blasphemy.
- The Prophet of Islam never spoke of derogation.

- Given sufficient insight and creative imagination all verses of the Qur'an can be reconciled with each other.
- Derogation theory, being handled as it is, is defeating itself.
- When the Qur'an speaks of replacing verses, it refers to the partial derogation by the Qur'an of previously revealed norms in the *Bible*.

EARLY EDITIONS

As described above, the Qur'an content-wise was fixed as early as 632.

This is, however, not true of its appearance, its *gestalt*. This is due to the fact that Arabic script in the 7th century was still underdeveloped. Some letters could only be read, or rather guessed, in context. The short vowels were not written at all. Nor had the so-called diacritical signs (al-tashkil; naqt al-'ijam) been invented for indicating, e.g., the absence of vowels between two consonants (as-sukun), the doubling of consonants (ash-shadda) or glottal stops (al-hamza).

As a mere memory aid the earliest Kufic script served well those who knew the Qur'an by heart. But when used for writing letters it might allow various readings. Muhammad Hamidullah even believed that the assassination of 'Uthman, the 3rd Caliph, was due to defective Kufi writing. A letter of his to the governor of Egypt had been intercepted. It should have been read:

"When he [the letter's bearer] comes to you, bid him welcome !"
It was, however read "When he comes to you, kill him !", causing outrage against such perfidy. The fatal mistake was made because the imperatives of "to welcome" (qabala) and "to kill" (qatala) were written identically.

Kufic writing—with its long horizontal lines—looked solid, quiet, and heavy. The Arabic scripts developed since look busy, elegant, and seem to be dancing above and below the line. As used for writing the Qur'an Arabic script cannot be topped in terms of precision. In contrast to the old Kufic script it no longer allows reciting the Qur'an in different dialects.

The development of Arab letters can be traced as follows: First one began to indicate vowels by adding thick dots (al-naqt al-i'rab), mainly in red. Dots were also used to distinguish between consonants, like "b" and "n" or "f" and "q" that previously had looked alike. This technique was already used in letters sent by 'Umar. During the reign of Malik al-Marwan (685-705), the 5th Damascus-based Umayyad Caliph, one started to apply double dots, in blue, green, yellow and orange color. Finally one introduced short oblique strokes, simple and double, for indicating short vowels and endings like – an, –in or –un. The last diacritical sign invented was the small circle that indicates an absence of vowels (as-sukun).

One has to admit that the availability of diacritical signs not only improved the readability but also the aesthetic possibilities of Arab calligraphy. Aside from the script, modern versions of the Qur'an have been rendered more useful by adding the names of the Surahs, listing the number of their verses and the place of revelation, i.e. either Mecca or al-Madinah. As well the Qur'anic text was divided into (numbered) verses, parts, sections and sub-sections. Those passages of the Qur'an which demand prostration when read (sajda al-tilawa) are indicated on the margin of the relevant pages.

In sum: Modern versions of the Qur'an are so precise that correct recitation is assured. However, even now the Qur'anic text is free of punctuation marks like period and comma, question, exclamation and quotation marks. This is prudent because punctuation marks might amount to a restriction of the possible variant meanings of a particular text. Therefore one can still read the word "ma" either as interrogative or as negation.

THE STRUCTURE OF THE QUR'AN

If one treats the Qur'an as an integrated whole it is entirely consistent.

– Neal Robinson

FORMAL ORGANIZATION
1. PARTS, SURAHS, VERSES

The Qur'an is subdivided into 114 chapters called "Surahs" (as-suar; sing. as-surah) containing altogether 6236 verses (al-ayat; sing. al-ayah). The entire text, comprising 77.437 words, has been equally divided into 30 parts (al-ajaz; sing. al-juz), 60 sections (al-ahzab; sing. al-hizb), and 120 sub-sections (al-arba´; sing. al-ruba´). This allows one to recite the Qur'an in equal portions, for instance during each day of the month of Ramadan.

Surahs and verses are of very different length. The shortest surahs –numbered 103, 108 and 110–consist of only three short verses. The 2nd surah, al-Baqara, is the longest one by far. Its 286 verses cover 1/12th of the entire Qur'an. Some verses consist of a single word, even a single letter (38: 1; 50: 1; 68: 1). Consequently some surahs with many verses–like the 26th one with its 227 verses–are much shorter than other surahs with fewer verses. If measured by verses one comes to the middle of the Qur'anic text in the 27th surah, if by words in the 18th surah.

2. NAMES

The names given to the surahs are man-made, not part of their revelation. This explains why some surahs are known under several names. This is true for surahs 9, 17, 35, 40, 41, 76, 83, 94, 96, 99, 106, 111, and 112. Except for Surah 112 the names chosen are found within their text or at their very beginning, like "Taha Ha" and "Ya Sin".

The 2nd Surah (al-Baqara) probably was named "Cow" because this word appears in this surah only, and that four times.

On the whole, when one looks for content the surah names are not helpful.

Only in case of surahs 4 ("Women") and 12 ("Joseph") do names and content fully correspond.

Not only surahs but also some verses have been given names. This is true for the Throne Verse (ayat al-kursi; 2: 255), the Light Verse (ayat an-nur; 24: 35), the Sword Verse (ayat as-saif; 9: 5) and the Hijab Verse (ayat al-hijab; 33: 35).

3. BASMALA

The Qur'an instructed Muslims to say "in the name of God!" (bismillah!) whenever beginning something, be it eating or driving or sleeping. Also the surahs of the Qur'an open with the "Basmala" (*bismillahi-r-rahmani-r-rahim*), i.e. in the name of God, the Benevolent, the Merciful.

In each case the basmala is part of the Qur'an but only in case of the 1st Surah, al-Fatiha, also its first verse. The Hanbali school of jurisprudence disagrees with that. Therefore, imams in Mecca and al-Madinah start the vocal recitation of al-Fatiha with what for others is its second verse: *al-hamduli-llahi rabbi-l-'alamin* (praised by God, Lord of the universe).

Only one surah, the 9th, is not opened by the *basmala*. This unique feature may indicate that the 9th surah content-wise is a continuation of the preceding one, even though it had been sent down seven years later than the 8th surah. Or the *basmala* may be missing here because the 9th surah mainly deals with warfare. After all, also when slaughtering an animal Muslims only pronounce the beginning of the *basmala*, dropping the reference to mercy and benevolence.

4. CHRONOLOGICAL ORDER

The surahs have been put in order as instructed by the Prophet. To put them into chronological order would not have been feasible since many surahs are composites from different periods. Nor would it have made good sense since the Qur'an is not a narrative. In as much as it refers to historical events it does so in an archetypical fashion, drawing lessons, not depicting history.

In addition, the Qur'an was not written in order to be read but to be recited.

For that purpose, each surah is a complete unit. It is repetitive for the reader, yes, but not for the Muslims who only hear small portions of the Qur'an when recited during prayer.

Nevertheless, much Muslim research has gone into dating of the surah and their composites, if only to resolve the question of derogation, already discussed.

In some cases dating was easy. There is agreement that the Qur'anic revelation began with 96: 1-5, surah 68 (beginning), surah 74 (beginning), surah 73 (beginning) and surah al-Fatiha, and that it ended with 5: 3, surah 110, and 2: 281.

One chronological listing of the surahs supposedly goes back to Ibn Abbas, one of the most knowledgeable companions of the Prophet. Inconsistent with it is the listing by Muhammad b. Nu'man b. Bashir found in Muhammad b. Ishaq b. an-Nadim`s 10th century literary guide "Al-Fihrist". To make matters worse, the modern standard edition of the Qur'an, the King Fu`ad edition of 1918/1925, offers a chronological list which neither agrees with the one by Ibn Abbas nor the one by Ibn Bashir. (The Cairo list is reproduced below at the end.) According to this listing only three surahs are placed where they should be chronologically: No. 38, 71 and 82.

I suspect that the various chronological sequences proposed differ for reasons of legal policy. By ranking a text as revealed later one might support its derogating power vis-à-vis an earlier text. In other words: I suspect that some of the dating supports the result of exegesis rather than being its basis.

Instead of reducing chronological uncertainties, Western Orientalists even increased them. Thus Theodor Nöldeke and his pupil Friedrich Schwally in their epochal "History of the Qur'an" (Geschichte des Qorans) disregarding

Muslim tradition proposed a new chronology based on topical, stylistic and linguistic (morphological) criteria. A century later, Richard Bell tried the same (1953). Yet all these attempts failed because at least 60 of the surahs contain matter both from the Meccan and the Medinan period.

Muslims are of course critical of attempts to attribute stylistic changes in the Qur'an to developments in the life of Muhammad. If, as they believe, God is the author linguistic maturation is excluded.

Muslims are also critical of circular logic. Orientalists for instance wrongly concluded that all references to God as "ar-Rahman" (the Merciful) date from the earliest period because God then frequently referred to Himself that way.

In sum: The longer Muslims tried to *date* surahs and verses the more they became convinced of the futility of the exercise. With *periodizing* it is a different story.

5. PERIODS

With Nöldeke and Schwally, without being overly precise, one can distinguish at least five Qur'anic periods:

- 1st Meccan Period characterized by highly poetic theological pronouncements, virtually gushing forth, with God referring to Himself as *ar-Rabb* (Master, Lord). Nöldeke allotted 48 surahs to this period. The same can, however, also be done with 60 (1, 17-21, 50-56, 67-109, 111-114).

- 2nd Meccan Period characterized by more extended rhythms, with God referring to Himself as *ar-Rahman* (the Merciful).
  One might allot 17 surahs to this period (29-32, 34-46).

- 3rd Meccan Period characterized by preaching and more regular end rhyming, now ending in –un and –in, God referring to Himself as *Allah*. 15 surahs may safely be allotted to this period (6, 7, 10-16, 22, 23, 25-28).

- Early Madinah Period characterized by its normativity. For it 9 surahs come into question (2, 3, 8, 47, 58, 59, 61, 62, 64).

• Late Madinah Period for which, too, normativity is typical. Probably it is represented by 13 surahs (4, 5, 9, 24, 33, 48, 49, 57, 60, 63, 65, 66, 110).

The Meccan surahs of the 1st and 2nd period are all to be found in the second half of the Qur'an, those of the 3rd period in is first half. The surahs from the Medinah Periods are, however, distributed over the entire Qur'an. One should therefore be happy enough with a rather rough periodization.

Even for that there is no guarantee.

6. Ordering by Length

It is normally taken for granted that the Qur'an is organized according to the length of its chapters since supposedly this was the Arab method for arranging anthologies. It is therefore assumed that the (mostly short) Meccan surahs are *all* found at the end and the (mainly long) Madinah ones are *all* in front. Nothing but misconceptions!

No written anthology of Arab poetry preceded the Qur'an as a possible model. Also, Arab anthologies were not arranged according to length but according to the end rhyme, i.e. alphabetically. Finally, it is simply not true that length was crucial for ordering the Qur'an. It begins and ends with short surahs.

If they had been ordered by length the large ones would have to be re-ordered as follows: 2, 4, 3, 7, 6, 5, 9. The 8th surah would be ranked in 20th position. The shortest surahs at the end as well are not ordered by length, otherwise they would appear in the following order: 102, 109, 107, 105, 111, 113, 114, 110, 106, 112, 103, 108.

Even though precise dating is not possible, there is no doubt that one finds Medinan surahs right next to Meccan ones, both in the first and in the second half of the Qur'an. At any rate, the official classification of surahs "revealed in Mecca" (86 surahs with 4613 verses) or "revealed in Madinah" (28 surahs with 1623 verses) is not fully reliable.

Needless to say that Zayd b. Thabit and the other companions of the Prophet would have been capable of ordering the Qur'an according to length. They respected the ordering given by the Prophet because it, too, was *revealed*.

If (because) this is so the Qur'an must be of a logical coherence subject to analysis. It was indeed discovered that many surahs are topically related to neighboring ones: Themes found at the end of a surah are resumed at the beginning of the following one. This is the case, for instance, with the last phrase of the 1st surah and the 1st verse of the 2nd surah. 3: 195 is connected with 4: 1 and 5: 120 with 6: 1. The same is true for the last verse of the 9th and the 3rd verse of the 10th surah.

7. ALTERNATIVE ORGANIZATION ?

Having described above the collection and edition of the one and only authentic version of the Qur'an, it seems contradictory now to admit that 'Abdallah Ibn Masud, one of the most renowned experts of the Qur'an, was in possession of an alternative, private version (Talif ibn Masud) in which three surahs were missing (1, 113, 114); also the internal order differed from the official one. 'Ubbay b. Ka'b as well maintained a private *mushaf* in which the 4th surah preceded the 3rd one, as it did in Ibn Masud's collection.

This riddle is solved if one realizes that both Ibn Masud and Ibn Ka'b had recorded their surahs in the order in which they had heard the Prophet recite them occasionally. Theirs are not alternative versions of the Qur'an but historical records of the Prophet's recital practice.

ORGANIZATION BY CONTENT

1. MAJOR THEMES

Except for the two surahs whose names indicate content there is no obvious thematic organizational principle behind the ordering of the Qur'an. On the contrary, one and the same topic may be treated repeatedly, in different surahs. Repetition helps highlighting subjects with increasing intensity. It was unavoidable any way given that each surah is a recitable closed unit. Therefore in case of the Qur'an it is more useful to consult its subject index than the table of contents.

Even so it is feasible to group major statements of the Qur'an around a few topics. This was already done in the 12th century CE by the magnificent Abu Hamid al-Ghazali. His scheme singled out six topics:

- information about God
- instructions for the way to Him
- definition of the human condition (conditio humana)
- lessons from history
- refutation of disbelief
- rules of life

Fazlur Rahman ("Major Themes of the Qur'an") in 1980 arrived at nine Qur'anic focal points:

- God
- nature
- man
- prophets
- life after death
- evil
- the Islamic community
- people of the book (Ahl al-Kitab), i.e. Jews and Christians
- religious pluralism

"Nature" stands for a number of amazingly correct scientific observations in the Qur'an, an unparalleled specificity of this script. When the Qur'an speaks God`s "signs" (ayat) reference is not only made to its verses but also to natural phenomena, since God manifests Himself both in His book and in His universe.

2. "TEN COMMANDMENTS"

As far as "rules of life" are concerned, the Qur'an is a thoroughly moralistic book that calls itself "guidance" (al-huda) teaching man how to deal with God, his environment, and himself. Statements on ethics virtually appear in every surah.

Even so only 17: 22-39 more or less corresponds to the Biblical Ten Commandments. These verses command Muslims to

- adore God alone, no other deity
- respect, honor, and take care of parents
- repent
- trust in God
- let babies live, wanted or unwanted
- stay clear of fornication and adultery
- protect human life
- be modest in revenge
- protect orphans
- keep contracts
- use correct weights and measurements
- mind their own business
- be modest.

Similarities to the ethics of other religions are not accidental.

3. STRUCTURAL ANALYSIS

Muslims as well as sensitive and emphatic Orientalists like Jacques Berque always surmised that the Qur'an was structured internally like a musical canon or a fugue.

In particular, Neal Robinson measured Qur'anic texts "isochronically", giving emphasized syllables two points and those without accent just one. When applied to the very first revelation–96: 1-5–this method rendered the following verse values: 12 : 10 : 8 : 10 : 12. Robinson had discovered an intricate symmetry of sound.

He was indeed convinced that God had used different sound registers when expressing (a) polemics, (b) eschatology, (c) instructions to Muhammad, (d) prophetic history, (e) God`s signs in nature and (f) the validity of His revelation. One can imagine how many other structural elements might come to light through computer analysis.

In the meantime research by Hamid Farahi, Amin Islahi and Angelika Neuwirth demonstrated that the composition (al-nizam) of the Qur'an is indeed internally coherent. This is not only true for the verse arrangement within surahs and their sequence but also for their sound pattern. Meaning, sound, color, linguistic rhythm, verbal morphology, and formal structure of the Qur'an are indeed cohesive.

The Indian pundit Hamid ad-Din Farahi (1863-1930) was the first researcher to suggest that the sequence of both surahs and verses was of enormous importance for understanding the Qur'an. For him not only the Qur'an as a whole but each individual surah presented an organic whole developed around a number of central themes (al-'amud). Rather intuitively Farahi divided the Qur'an into nine groups.

His young collaborator Amin Ahsan Islahi (1904-1997), Indian Muslim as well, in his nine volume "contemplative" Qur'an commentary in Urdu, *Taddabur-i-Qur'an*, considerably extended the Farahi approach. In the process, he came to the conclusion that all surahs (except 1, 24 and 33) thematically form pairs: The preceding surah introducing a topic, the following one illustrating or varying it.

This structure can be demonstrated for surahs 2+3, 4+5, 6+7 and 8+9. Other surahs are less obviously paired.

Instead of nine, Islahi isolated seven groups of surahs, each group beginning with a (rather theoretical) Meccan surah and ending with a (rather more practical) Medinan one:

Group 1:	Surahs 1-5	Topic: Legal order
Group 2:	Surahs 6-9	Topic: The Abrahamic religions
Group 3:	Surahs 10-24	Topic: Truth / Error
Group 4:	Surahs 25-33	Topic: Role of the Prophet
Group 5:	Surahs 34-49	Topic: God`s unity
Group 6:	Surahs 50-66	Topic: Life after death
Group 7:	Surahs 67-114	Topic: Warning disbelievers

Structural analysis certainly is crucial for understanding the meaning of the Qur'an; but it is not the only access. In fact, breaking the Qur'anic text down into thematic groups is rather subjective. Some surahs, though, definitely focus on leitmotifs:

- The "opening" 1st Surah, al-Fatiha, the first surah revealed as a unit, with its "frequently recited seven verses" is an essential component of Muslim ritual prayer, being recited 17 times each day. Al-Fatiha concisely addresses all the core subjects of the Qur'an.

- The longest surah, al-Baqara (no. 2), the first surah revealed in al-Madinah, contains the entire theology of the Qur'an and most of its ethical rules. It therefore deserves the name "Mother of the Qur'an" (umm al-Qur'an).

- While the 2nd surah extensively deals with Judaism, the 3rd surah focuses on Christianity.

- The 4th surah (an-Nisa) in accordance with its name mainly discusses women and family issues.

- The 5th surah contains the nutritional rules of Islam.

- The 36th surah is read to people when dying.

- The 112th surah (al-Ikhlas /Sincerity) is a manifesto of *at-tawhid*, the belief in God's unity and uniqueness. According to a saying of the Prophet this very short surah is equivalent to one-third of the Qur'an.

- The 113th and 114th surahs play a particular role as "protective surahs".

THE LANGUAGE OF THE QUR'AN

Poetics serves rhetoric and rhetoric serves religion.

— Kenneth Cragg

POETIC BEAUTY

No language, not even French, is more revered than Arabic. Some Muslims basing themselves on 12: 2, 16: 103 and 26: 195 continue to believe that Arabic is "God's own language", created by Him (tawqif al-lughat). Others draw a parallel to the Jewish notion of the Chosen People when stating that Arabic was God's Chosen Language.

At any rate, in pre-Islamic Arabia Arabic was the only highly developed cultural product, poetry being the only known art form. The Arabs with their lyrics had begun to turn their world into language. Their civilization was textual (Abu Zaid). If Jesus' field of action was healing and magic the one of Moses, the domain of Islam was linguistics (Bamyeh).

Therefore it was quite natural (and not necessarily insulting) for the Meccans to suspect that Muhammad in essence was a poet (69: 40f.; 52: 30).

It was wrong to insinuate that Muhammad had thought up the Qur'an, but it was correct to acknowledge its lyrical qualities. Since the style of the Qur'an broke with many Arab tradition, their flattery was even more remarkable.

As God's Word the Qur'an is not literature in the normal sense. Nor can it, for instance, be profanely categorized as "rhymed prose". However, the Qur'an, too, is accessible only because it follows the laws of aesthetics and grammar of classical Arabic. Indeed, no chef d'oeuvre of world literature impressed readers as deeply as the Qur'an keeps doing. Otherwise, as an unaccessible divine super-idiom it could only be used ritually, like magic.

In sum, it is permissible to analyze the stylistic and linguistic specificities of the Qur'an. In fact, one cannot help but distinguish differences, like the one between the highly poetic, intense and powerful language of the earliest surahs and the drawn-out and measured style of the later ones. (In Mecca the issue was to find believers, in al-Madinah to guide them.) Remarkably, computer analysis near Paris confirmed that the language in both periods belongs to one and the same author. In fact, Muhammad's language profile derived from the collection of his sayings (al-ahadith) does not jibe with the Qur'anic one.

Of course, while arabo-phone Muslims can be fascinated by the mere beauty of the Qur'anic language; other Muslims rather marvel at its wisdom.

The formal beauty of the Qur'an is not only due to end rhyming and alliteration but also to assonance, word play, and internal rhythm. Providing below a transcription (with accents) of the 99th surah, I hope to give an idea of the formal beauty of much of the Qur'an. Its end rhyme "a" here marks the last three syllables. ("Dh" is to be pronounced like a voiced English "th", "th" like an unvoiced English "th"; "kh" like a gutteral German "ch" and "z" like a voiced "s".)

Idha zulzilât al-ard zilzâlahâ
wa akhrashât al-ard athqâlahâ
wa qâla-l-insân mâ lahâ ?
yaum idhin tuhâdithu akhbârahâ
bi-anna râbbaka awhâlahâ
yaum idhin jasduru-n-nâs ashtâtan li-yuru ʿamâlahum:
fâ mân yâmalu mithqâla dhârratin khâiran yârahu
fâ mân yâmalu mithqâla dhârratin shârran yârahu.

In English:

When the earth is shaken with its shaking,
and the earth throws out its burden,
and man cries: What is the matter with her ?
On that day she will tell her story
as inspired by her Lord.

On that day people will come forward singly to see their
deeds.
So who does good equal to the weight of an atom will see it.
So who does wrong equal to the weight of an atom will see it.

This surah in addition to rhyme and rhythm displays another
stylistic pecularity: interjected verses. Verse 6 sounds as if it had been
inserted belatedly by way of commentary. One might as well put it in
parentheses. Or so one thinks.

In reality the 99th surah is of a piece, simultaneously revealed. Far
from being a non sequitur , the interjection in Verse 6 through an
aesthetic shock produces a mini-break for reflection.

Surah 97 is equally impressive:

Inna ânzalnahu fi lâilat al-qâdr
Wa ma adrâka ma lâilat al-qâdr
Lâilat al-qadri khâirun min alf shâhr
Tanazalû al-malâika wa-r-rûh fiha bi-idhni
râbbihim min kulli âmr
Salâm hiya hâtta matlâ`i-l-fâjr

In English:
Verily, We sent it down in the Fateful Night.
And what will let you know what is the Fateful Night ?
The Fateful Night is better than a thousand months.
The angels and the spirit come down in it by permission of
their Lord, for all purposes.
Peace it is until the rising of dawn.

Bishop Kenneth Cragg ("The Event of the Qur'an") is probably right
in alleging that authentic revelation, being art without artificiality, is
always poetic.

OATHS AND CURSES

In Arabic "*wa*" means "and". Used in front of a noun "wa" may,
however, turn into a particle of conjuration. "And the sun!", for instance,

would have to be translated "By the sun !". "Wa" in such cases leads to a confirmation by oath.

In the Qur'an quite a few of the older surahs begin this way, i.e. the surahs number 68, 75, 77, 79, 85, 86, 89, 91, 92, 93, 95 and 103. In these cases God verifies the truth of His statements by associating them with something else that undoubtedly is true. Thus we read: **By the night as it envelopes!** (92: 1) or **By the fig and the olive!** (95: 1) or **By the time !** (103:1).

It is conspicuous that God never swears by Himself nor by non-sensual, abstract matters. This led Bint al-Shati to see these oaths as stylistic tricks gaining attention for what follows.

On the other hand, Angelika Neuwirth sees no conjuration involved at all. Indeed, the formula "lâ uqsimu" with which seven of the mentioned surahs begin can be reads as "Indeed I swear..." or—on the contrary—as "I do not swear", all depending on whether "lâ" is seen as accentuation or negation.

In some cases, the Qur'an seems to embody divine curses: **Accursed be the conjecturers (51: 10); So let him be cursed, how he plotted!** (74: 19) or **Cursed be man, how ungrateful he is!** (80: 17). This is, however, doubtful because in each case the verb used (3rd person; perfect tense; passive) cannot only be read optatively but as indicating a completed action.Thus, for instance, *qutila* may not mean "Be he killed!" but simply, narratively, "he has been killed". So there may be no swearing at all.

ALLEGORIES AND METAPHORS

The Qur'an discusses metaphysical subjects like God, angels, djinn, heaven and hell—for which all languages are inept. It does not take a Ludwig Wittgenstein to realize that Arabic, too, developed through the naming of visible or audible sensual objects, is unsuitable for metaphysical subjects. The Qur'an admits this dilemma by speaking in images and parables (al-mathal, sing. al-mithl). In the Light Verse (24: 59) God points out that His light is a metaphor.

That the Qur'an can deal with the invisible (al-ghayb) is due indeed to its tropical method, i.e. its use of allegories and metaphors. Abstract, non-sensual phenomena are made concrete with the help of images familiar to us. This is dangerous only if one forgets that we are dealing with similes and simulacra of our own making. In that case we become victims of anthropologizing the divine.

It is therefore essential to remain conscious of the truism that we cannot grasp any of the ultimate realities, even if we recite the 99 (or more) "most beautiful names" of God (al-asma al-husna; 17: 110), i.e. His attributes, many of which are found in 59: 22-24. There God is called the Omniscient, Merciful, Beneficent, Lord, Holy, Savior, Guardian, Majestic, Compeller, Supreme, Creator, Founder, Formgiver, Mighty, and the Wise.

We can comprehend this self-description of God only if we can associate it with experiences made by ourselves. Which amounts to saying that we cannot comprehend God since all of our experiences are tied to the categories of time and space.

One way out of this dilemma is to use God's "names" nominalistically "without asking how" (bi-la kaifa), as suggested in the 10th century CE already by the Ash'ariyya philosophical school in Baghdad. Nominalistic as well has to be our handling of terms like Doomsday and Last Judgement (yaum id-din) when the Last Hour (as-sa'at) has come and the doors of Heaven (al-jannah) and Hell (al-jahannam) open–notwithstanding the fact that the Qur'an is deceivingly descriptive of the undescribable:

When the stars are put out
and when the sky is cleft asunder
and when the mountains are blown away...
(77: 8-10; also see 82: 1-5)

How to read the vivid descriptions of the invisible world of bliss and suffering in heaven and hell? There is only one way: To interpret such texts as allegories and forego quibbling about details. Such descriptions are less a map of the other world than a way of motivating our behavior here.

Reading the Qur'an we find very absorbing accounts of the Garden of Eden: deep, saturated greenery; cool shade; bubbling springs of water (76: 6); palm trees bursting with dates, and pomegranates (55: 68); female companions with big dark eyes, clad in satin (52: 20; 55: 72; 56: 22), and boys-in-waiting, eternally young (56: 17). Such luxuries not only appeal to the Bedouin audience to which the Qur'anic message originally was addressed. How else could God have depicted paradise to people suffering of tropical heat and lack of water?

The Qur'anic images of Heaven and Hell alternate, often quite abruptly and with threatening overtones. 52: 13-27 is a good example for such a diptych.

Some readers feel uncomfortable with such drastic eschatological paintings.

Well, that is exactly their point. It takes big caliber rhetorical guns to shock lethargic people out of their complacency, crude materialism, and anything-goes-mentality. It certainly does not hurt to face up to one's mortality well before one breathes one's last.

At any rate, the Qur'anic method of alarming people was highly effective. Many Meccans changed their evil ways overnight. Islam brought about an early cultural revolution. The Muslims in Mecca and al-Madinah during the lifetime of their charismatic Prophet were historically unique as a community always ready in total confidence to sacrifice their property, their limbs and life for the cause of Islam. The Qur'an had fueled a heroism that frequently reflected a zeal for the promised life after death.

Were they, or are we, naïve ?

CLEAR AND VEILED

Allegories and metaphors in the Qur'an must be distinguished from passages which are enigmatic, i.e. dark, or carry several meanings—open (zahir) or hidden (batin) ones. In case of allegories and metaphors it is obvious that they must not be taken literally. In case of veiled verses this is not at all obvious.

For people particularly fond of *esoteric* speculation–*batinists*– the Qur'an is a rich field. However, if we leave its esoteric meaning, do we not lose all ground under out feet? Where is the net? It is one thing to be in awe of the Lord and His revelation (39: 23) and to believe in the unseen (2: 3). Trying to pierce the veil between the visible and the invisible world (al-ghayb) is a different (and arrogant) story.

Esoteric commentaries of the Qur'an are normal in the Shi´ite world and Sufi circles, as typified by Muhy ad-Din ibn al-´Arabi. In seeking hidden meanings they do exactly what the Qur'an urged them to leave alone (3: 7).

SPECIFICS OF GRAMMAR

In the Qur'an one finds a number of grammatical peculiarities which should be maintained in translation:

(1) Incomplete (elliptical) interrogative sentences.

Being rhetorical, they must be completed by the reader. Example: **"Is he who will face the awful torment on the Day of Resurrection?"** (39: 24).

(2) Incomplete indications of time. This is the case when sentences simply begin with "when he said:" (idha qala).

(3) Past tense for future events. If a future event is certain, it can be expressed in past tense because it is as if it had already happened.

(4) Change of grammatical person (al-iltifat). Mainly with reference to God as the speaker there are abrupt changes of the subject

- from 1st to 2nd person (but not in reverse)
- from 3rd to 1st person (and in reverse)
- from 3rd to 2nd person
- from singular to plural
- from one addressee to another.

There may be several changes in a row (70: 39-41) and, in case of verbs, also of tense. Examples:

- In the 1st surah God is the grammatical subject, however, in verses 1-4 in 3rd person singular (He, Him) and from verse 5 in second person (You, Your).

- 10: 21 reads: "*Our messengers record all that you plot.*" Verse 22 continues: "*He it is Who...*"
- In 35: 27 there is such a change within the same verse: "*Do you not see that Allah sends down water from the sky, and therewith We produce fruit.*"

To be sure, nothing in the Qur'an is fortuitous, by mere chance. Therefore, it was unwarranted for Orientalists like Theodor Nöldeke to treat grammatical *peculiarities* as *irregularities*, i.e. as mistakes, rather than–like Jacques Berque–as special features with special functions.

When God speaks in the 1st person singular (I) or with *pluralis majestatis* (We) He underscores His majesty and nearness: "*Am I not your Lord?*" In that case His communication is *expressive*.

When God speaks in the 2nd person singular as "*Your Lord*" the accent is on His audience. In that case His communication is *connective*.

When God is referred to in the 3rd person singular (He, Allah) the accent is on the message. This communication of His is *cognitive*.

SPECIFICS OF LINGUISTICS

1. Vocabulary: The language of the Qur'an makes little use of adjectives. It is, however, rich in verbs and employs them in all of their eight possible modalities, frequently in the form of gerund ("*having heard*"). The verbal use of substantives ("*they will be the victorious ones*") is quite common, so is the passive voice of verbs.

On the whole, the Qur'an uses few tenses–mainly the present and the imperfect tense–and a simple, even modest vocabulary–not the sophisticated, rare, and intellectual stock of words used in Arabic poetry. In particular, verbs are scarce whose roots (al-masdar) have four syllables. Only 15 of them have been identified in the Qur'an, even though pre-Islamic poets were fond of using a large number of them.

Of course, the apparent simplicity of the Qur'anic language is misleading. It hides many layers of meaning.

2. Duplication: In Arabic it is rhetorically effective if one and the same word is used more than once in the same sentence. (In European

languages one must avoid such "unaesthetic" duplication.) Examples: "If the earth is shaken with its shaking" (*Idha zulzilat al-ard zilzalaha* 99: 1) and: "Is the reward of goodness other than goodness ?" (55: 60).

3. Onomatopoeia: The Qur'an likes to use words whose sound is suggestive of their meaning.

4. Alliteration: Frequently employed, as in 114: 4 f.: "...*waswasi khannas alladhi yuwaswisu fi...* The very first Qur'anic revelation already was phonetically intricate, pairing words like: 'alaq / khalaq; iqra / ikram; and 'allam / ya'lam.

5. Dialogue: In several passages sentences seem to be comments on the previous ones. This is true of 4: 46 whose first sentence is explained by the second, as is the third by the fourth. Surah 16: 110 as well corresponds to that scheme a / b / a / b:

(a) **And when We change a revelation for another**

(b) **–and Allah knows best what He revealed–**

(a) **they say: >You are but inventing !<**

(b) **But most of them do not know.**

6. Refrain: There are passages in the Qur'an where recurring phrases suggest a dialogue. Prototypically this is the case with the 55th Surah ar-Rahman in which the interjection "Which of the blessings of your Lord will you deny?" appears 32 times.

7. Pathos and Emphasis: Many Qur'anic phrases begin with a pathetic *wa* ("and" or "but") or with *inna* or *qad* ("indeed", "truly", "certainly"), all designed to add emphasis.

8. "Wa": The Arabic word for "and" is not only used emphatically. In most cases it simply connects two phrases. This is done so frequently that Arabic can be accused of suffering from wa-ism. Nor see Arab speakers any contradiction in combing "and" with "but". Dozens of Qur'anic phrases begin with *wa lakin* ("And however,").

9. Ambivalence (al-ibham): That words carry several meanings is typical for all languages. This is even true of key Qur'anic concepts like *ayah* (sign; verse) and *din* which can mean religion, faith, submission, solidarity, legal judgement, rite or way of life. Therefore the same word

should not always be translated the same way. Arabic may, however, be the only language that uses words with contradictory, mutually exclusive meanings. One and the same term may mean "dusk" or "dawn". In such cases a Qur'anic verse can be understood in one or the other way, or both ways.

10. Synonyms: There is no agreement among experts on the existence of synonyms in the Qur'an. Indeed, what seems exchangeable at first sight often is not upon reflection. Therefore it is not advisable simply to explain one Qur'anic word by another.

11. Gender-neutral vocabulary: The concept of "God" (al-ilah; Allah) in Arabic is gender-neutral. Even though Allah in the Qur'an frequently refers to Himself as "He" (huwa), it remains clear that God must not be classified as masculine or feminine. This delegitimizes as well Muslim feminist attempts to translate huwa as "Her". Surprisingly a few other Arabic key terms are genderless as well. This is true, and makes good sense, of "spouse" (zawj) and companion (huri). Consequently, the Qur'an is much less male-oriented than mostly assumed.

12. Addressees: The Qur'an addresses itself to the following:
   • mankind (ayuha-n-nas !)
   • believers / Muslims (ayuha-l-mu`minun / muslimun !)
   • Muhammad (ayuha-n-nabiyu !)
   • disbelievers (ayuha-l-kafirun !)
   • polytheists (al-mushrikun)
   • hypocrites (al-munafiqun)

Whether Christians are to be classified among polytheists depends on whether they interpret "Trinity" as a union of three divine persons or as one God with multiple manifestations.

"Disbelievers" is a necessary while unsatisfactory classification. Literally a kafir (pl. al-kufar) is someone who puts (the truth) under a blanket, i.e. someone who rejects faith in spite of knowing better. Whenever the Qur'an speaks of believers or unbelievers both men and women are targeted. This is well demonstrated in the famous verse 33: 35 :

Indeed, men who submit to God, and women who submit
to God, and men who believe and women who believe, and
men who obey and women who obey, and truthful men and
truthful women, and men who are patient and women who are
patient, and men who are humble and women who are humble,
and men who are charitable and women who are charitable,
and men who fast and women who fast, and men who guard
their chastity and women who guard their chastity, and men
who remember God and women who remember God–God
has prepared for them forgiveness and a vast reward

ENIGMAS

29 of the 114 surahs begin with enigmatic, unrelated letters (al-
muqatta'at). These appear as single letters (surahs 38, 50, 68) or in combinations of up to five letters. The first two verses of the 42th Surah
consist of such letter combinations only. The 19th Surah is unique in
being opened by a group of five letters (K H Y 'A S), the largest
number of letters in Arabic word roots (al-masdar). It has been observed
that only 14 letters appear in the Muqatta'at, which is exactly half of the
Arabic alphabet.

In two instances the same letter combinations open a group of surahs.
This is true of surahs 40-46 ("Ha Mim") and surahs 10-14 and 15 ("Alif
Lam Ra"). In can be disputed whether the letters "Ta Ha" before surah 20
and "Ya Sin" before surah 36 are "unconnected letters" at all. *Ta Ha* and
Ya Sin could indeed mean "Oh, man !".

Muhammad never volunteered any explanation of the Muqatta'at,
nor did his companions inquire about it.

Of course, later on Muslims were more intrigued by this phenomenon, given that it is without parallel. An enormous amount of ingenuity
was invested in solving the Muqatta'at riddle, especially by Qur'an
commentators like al-Tabari. Only a few of them, including Muhammad
Hamidullah, voiced the opinion that there is nothing to explain , only to
accept. Personally, I should rather side with commentators like Yusuf Ali

and Muhammad Asad who do see a riddle, but one which will never be solved.

Over time, the following hypotheses have been advanced:

• The unconnected letters are the initials of scribes who wrote down the surahs in question. This (typically Orientalist) thesis must be excluded because the Prophet always included the Muqatta'at when reciting.

• The letters refer to the numerological value of the surahs in question. This is an un-Islamic, Cabbalistic way of of looking at texts.

• The letters are abbreviations of divine attributes ("names"). If so, according to the sectarian Muhammad 'Ali, "ra" could stand for ra'i (the Seer). Ibn 'Arabi, the great mystic, saw "A L M" as standing in for Allah, Logos, and Muhammad and "H M" for *habibi Muhammad* ("my friend Muhammad"). Limitless fantasy.

• The letters are magical seals, sealing their surahs. This is circular magic, explaining one secret by another.

• The letters are conjuration, solemnly assuring the veracity of the following text (Theodor Nöldeke). This is not plausible since none of the short surahs carry unconnected letters.

• The letters are provisionally given surah names. If so, why were they retained after the surahs had received their standard names?

• The letters are a rhetorical means (or trick) to obtain heightened attention–an undignified explanation, to say the least.

• Kenneth Cragg suggested that the Muqatta'at were symbolic raw material of eloquence–whatever that might mean.

• Recently Angelika Neuwirth wondered whether the enigmatic letters might be a key to the understanding and positioning of their surahs. She noted all surahs carrying such letters somehow deal with the phenomenon of revelation. But so do many others.

Sum total: Muslims would be on the safe side if they considered the enigmatic letters as belonging to those ambivalent verses (al-mutashabihat) from whose hidden meanings they should stay clear because God alone knows their significance (3: 7).

INIMITABILITY

> If the Qur'an had been similar to other books, it would have
> lacked the force to impact on the Arabs the way it did.
>   –Rashid Rida, Al-Wahy al-Muhammad

The Qur'an thanks to is origin (revelation) and content was not
only Muhammad's "accrediting miracle" but the only miracle (al-
mu'jiza) recognized by all Muslims. In 17: 88 the Qur'an proclaims its
own inimitability (al-'ijaz). In fact, in some provocative (tahaddi)
verses the Qur'an challenges its readers to come up with a similar text,
even one single surah (2: 23; 10: 38)–knowing that they will be unable
to do so (11: 13; 28: 49; 52: 34). According to Navid Kerman it is
a fascinating facet of the Islamic religion that with the Qur'an it
proposes an *aesthetic* proof of God. Whether these challenges refer
to the beauty of the Qur'anic language only or also to the *contents* of
the Book–its truth, compelling logic, coherence, completeness (6: 38;
16: 89) and wisdom–is under dispute.

There is indeed no other holy script which has shaped world history
as much and, in contrast to the Bible, continues to do so in modern times.

CREATED/UNCREATED

> Whether the Qur'an is eternal? This is not my question
> Whether the Qur'an is created? That I do not know.
> That it is the book of all books
> I dutifully believe as a Muslim.
>   – Johann Wolfgang von Goethe, West-Östlicher Divan

The Qur'an tells us that its original text, the Mother of the Book (umm al-kitab) and source of all revelation, is with God—well guarded on tablets (al-lauh al-mahfuz; 3: 7; 13: 39; 43: 4; 56: 78). It figures that God being eternal, i.e. not subject to change, His Word, too, must be eternal.

In the 9th century, in Baghdad, seat of the Abbasid caliphs, the thesis of the *uncreatedness* of the Qur'an was challenged in a philosophical dispute whose tragic consequences are still with us. Several caliphs sided with the so-called Mu`tazila School of Thought which, on purely rational grounds, alleged that the Qur'an had been *created*, in time. The conflict got out of hand when the Mu`tazila doctrine was officially enforced. Now Islam had its inquisition, preceding the Christian one by several centuries. The venerable founder of the Hanbalite School of Jurisprudence, Imam Ibn Hanbal, was not the only great Muslim intellectual thrown into prison for taking what temporarily was seen as the wrong side.

The counter-reaction, formulated by the so-called Ash'ariyya School of Thought, with the help of a conservative caliph gained strength, however, at an exorbitant price: From now on Muslims suspected all philosophy of being heretical or leading to heresy. Metaphysics became frowned upon in Islam. Abu Hamid al-Ghazali (d. 1111), himself the last great orthodox Muslim philosopher, endicted philosophy devastatingly with his anti-metaphysical chef d`oeuvre "The Contradiction of Philosophy" (al-tahafut al-falasifa).

Another consequence, following promptly, of the victory of the uncreatedness–doctrine were theological exaggerations. The Qur'an was now treated as "inlibration" of God, God virtually being present in His book.

In hindsight it is difficult to understand the passion that agitated the representatives of both Schools of Thought. Mu'tazila, and Ash'ariyya. After all, both sides proceeded from the same assumption: that the Qur'an is the word of God. Apparently the dispute had been caused by a classical misunderstanding: The Ash'ariyya focuses on the archetypal, timeless Qur'an as eternally the Word of God while the Mu'tazila focused on the historical, written Qur'an as a concrete event. So there is room for reconciliation.

Interpretation of The Qur'an

The Qur'an is a guide for all living beings on the planet
earth, a textbook for learning a new language
—the language of spirituality.
> – Muzaffar Haleem, *The Sun Rises in the West*, 1999

Methodology

Someone who deviates from the line taken by the companions of the Prophet (as-sahaba) or their immediate successors (at-tabi'un) when interpreting the Qur'an is in error. (Ibn Taymiyya)

1. Qualification: Strict as he was Imam Ibn Taymiyya even in the 13th century, 600 years after the Prophet, would only admit interpretation of the Qur'an (i) by itself, (ii) as given by the Prophet in his Sunnah, and (iii) by his companions and their immediate successors. He was not entirely against drawing conclusions by analogy. But he rejected the rationalistic approach (at-tafsir bi-r-ray) to exegesis applied by al-Zamakhshari, a famous commentator contemporary to him. Of course he was also critical of the esoteric approach of Sufis who seemed to make everything relative by reading between the lines.

Again, 700 years later, Shaykh Muhammad Abduh (d. 1905), one of the neo-rationalist authors of the influential Qur'an commentary *Tafsir al-Manar*, noted down: "On Judgement Day God will not ask us about how others understood the Qur'an. He will ask us about our own position." What a world of difference! At his time, Abduh's views were revolutionary. But today it is widely believed that each Muslim is not only entitled to his own Qur'an interpretation but obliged to pursue it.

Obviously, there must be a less dangerous middle-way between Ibn Taymiyya and Muhammad Abduh. Neither is it defensible to refuse interpretation nor should the "door of interpretation" (bab al-ijtihad) be thrown wide open, for everyone.

2. Literal Understanding: There are still many devout Christians and Muslims around who, as literalist fundamentalists, believe that Bible and Qur'an can be understood "as they are". Such literalists overlook that understanding even the simplest word is the result of (unconscious) interpretation. Without its context, the educational and experimental background of both addressor and addressee, and the epistemological history of the word in question it escapes comprehension.

3. Rules of Interpretation: The Qur'an contains rules for its own interpretation like the principle that different parts of the Qur'an explain each other (: al-Qur'an jufassir ba'duhu bi-ba'da). This amounts to a warning against interpreting out of context. Of course, this principle is not workable when expressions appear in the Qur'an just once (like as-samad in 112: 2).

The Qur'an even gives instructions on how to deal with its own dark or ambivalent passages:

He it is Who revealed to you the Book. In it are clear [muhkamat] verses–they are the mother [substance] of the book–and other, ambiguous [mutashabihat] ones. But those in whose hearts is doubt above all pursue that which is allegorical, seeking dissension by seeking to explain it. Nobody but God knows its explanation. And those with sound understanding say: We believe in it. One and the other are from God." (3: 7)

This truly fundamental rule has been altered fundamentally by Shi'ite Muslims. They do not stop at the next to last sentence after "explanation" but run it into the following one. As a result, they read: "Nobody but God knows its explanation and those with sound understanding. They say..."

With this sleight of hand it is implied that the members of the Prophet's family and their descendants have supra-natural access to the "true" meaning of the Qur'an.

4. Occasions for Revelation: One can only arrive at a correct understanding of what the Qur'an has to say about a given issue if

one knows the sequence of revelation of relevant verses. As Roman lawyers already recognized, in case of normative verses the knowledge of sequence is essential. This is so because a later general norm (lex posterior generalis) will suspend an earlier general norm (lex anterior generalis). The same is true for later specific norms (lex posterior specialis); they, too, alter or cancel earlier specific norms (les anterior specialis). Only specific and general norms can exist side by side, no matter which one precedes the other.

Muslim lawyers use these categories of Roman law but often do not have sufficient information on the sequence of revelation. To unearth more knowledge in this field was the task of the science of "occasions for revelation" (asbab al-nuzul). It would, however, be misleading to interpret the Qur'an primarily in the light of the occasions for revelation as if certain happenings would have caused a revelation, or as if problem-oriented revelations (khusus as-sabab) could not contain timeless messages as well.

The occasions for revelation are the interface between the Absolute and the particular. This can be well illustrated in connection with the marriage of the Prophet with Zaynab bint Jashash (33: 37): It presented the concrete occasion for the permanent ruling that orphaned children may not be legally adopted, treating them ficti-tiously as blood relatives. (Ever since, in the Muslim world orphans are not adopted but taken care of by foster parents.)

5. Team Work: It should be clear by now that commentators of the Qur'an must be expert in several fields, including Arabic, linguistics, and Islamic history. They must know the semantics of 7th century Arabia and pre-Islamic poetry, the life of the Prophet (as-sira) and his Sunnah, the views of earlier Qur'an commentators, the newest exploits of natural science ('ilm) and the problems that contemporary Muslims have to face.

Obviously, no single learned person can be in command of all that. Therefore, modern Qur'an commentaries require a number of specialists working together as a team.

QUR'AN AND SUNNAH

Essentially it is the function of the Sunnah to explain. And what explains is subordinate to what it explains (Taha Jabir al-'Alwani).

We have arrived now at the key question of how Qur'an and Sunnah relate to each other.

One extreme view sees Qur'an and Sunnah as two basic sources of equal rank, both rooted in divine intervention, be it revelation (Qur'an) or inspiration (Sunnah). If the Qur'an is God's Word written down, the Prophet "lived the Qur'an". Are Muslims not instructed by the Qur'an to obey both God and the Prophet? The late Shaykh al-Azhar, Gadd al-Haq 'Ali Gad al-Haqq, was representative of this viewpoint. If it was correct the Qur'an might have been derogated by the Sunnah, and this is indeed claimed in individual cases like the penalty for adultery.

In strong contrast, the Muslim majority admits of only one single primary source of Islam: the Qur'an. Not only is it primary in status, it is also authentic beyond any doubt. (The same cannot be said for the entire Sunnah.)

Consequently Taha Jabir al-'Alwani, former head of the prestigious International Institute of Islamic Thought (IIIT) in Herndon, Virginia (USA), maintains that the Sunnah can explain and supplement the Qur'an but never alter it. If this is so there simply cannot be any contradictions between Qur'an and Sunnah since the Qur'an always has the last word.

The explanatory function of the Sunnah is indeed indispensible. Book 60 of *Sahih al-Bukhari*, the famous hadith–collection by al-Bukhari, lists 358 explanations of Qur'anic verses given by the Prophet, covering no less than 5, 7% of the Qur'anic material.

At the same time, one must remain appreciative of the Sunnah's supplementary function. It is equally essential since the Qur'an failed to address many subjects or only dealt with them in general fashion. This is why–without the Prophet's Sunnah–the Muslims would not know how to pray, how to fast, how to perform pilgrimage. In fact, without the Sunnah Islam might have paled into a sort of Unitarian Deism.

Qur'an Translations

Only the Arabic text of the Qur'an deserves the name "Qur'an". Muslims always knew that translating it, no matter into which language, is highly problematic since translations willy-nilly are interpretations which cannot help reducing the semantic richness of the original. These effects cannot be avoided since no two languages possess vocabulary which is identical in meaning and all its associations.

This explains why it took 1100 years before Shaykh Walli Allah Dihlawi in Delhi (d. 1762) dared to prepare a Persian Qur'an translation, followed by a translation into Urdu by his two sons, Rafi'ad-Din and 'Abd al-Qadir, not printed until 1894.

Outside the Muslim world nobody had such qualms. Even so, the first translation of the Qur'an into a Western language, Latin, had to await 1143. As an illegitimate child of the Crusades its preparation was ordered by the Abbot of Cluny, Peter the Venerable (d. 1156), and realized in Toledo by Hermann of Dalmatia and Robert Kettenensis. But this translation in turn had to await its printing for another 400 years.

Suggested by Martin Luther and with a preface by him this first Latin version of the Qur'an was printed in 1543 by Theodor Bibliander in Basle. The Turkish campaigns into central Europe finally had prompted this printing.

Until the 18th century, translations of the Qur'an into English, French and German were re-translations from this Latin version, not directly based on the Arabic original.

Since then, the Qur'an has been translated into at least 65 languages, into English more than 40 times. Even so, it took again a long time before Western Muslims and Muslims living in the West —no longer Christian missionaries, Jews and Orientalists only—started translating the Qur'an as well. Prime examples for this development are translation into English by Marmaduke Pickthall, Yusuf Ali, Muhammad Asad, and Abdalhaqq / Aisha Bewley.

ARABIC QUR'AN COMMENTARIES

The Qur'an is self-explanatory and its own best commentator. Nevertheless, there is a great demand, and need, for expert introduction and guidance.

Non-expert Muslims are particularly thankful for being advised on

- possible alternative meanings
- concordant passages
- relevant explanatory traditions of the Prophet
- early commentaries
- time and place of, and occasions for, revelation (usul al-Qur'an)
- pre-Islamic conditions.

As long as the most knowledgeable companions and wives of the Prophet–like 'Abdullah ibn Abbas, 'Abdullah ibn Mas'ud, 'Ali ibn Abi Talib, Ubbay ibn Ka'b, Abu Ubayda, Zayd ibn Thabit, 'A`isha bint Abu Bakr—were alive there was no demand yet for written commentaries. As it was, these admirable people were walking commentaries of the Qur'an.

Ever since, though, commentaries in Arabic became increasingly important for the global development of Islam. The following eleven authors warrant listing in any anthology:

- Tabari, Abu Jafar Muhammad ibn Jarir al-, d. 923, Jami'al-Bayan 'an Tawil Ay al-Qur'an: a 30 volume, verse-by-verse classical commentary, currently translated into English. Traditional in its methodology (tafsir bi-l-ma`thur) it relies philologically on pre-Islamic poetry.
- Tustari, Sahl bin 'Abdullah Abu Muhammad, d. 896, Tafsir al-Qur'an al-'Azim : First commentary from a Sufi (mystical) perspective, proceeding from the assumption that the key Qur'anic messages are hidden, only to be understood by gnostic dervishes thanks to their illumination (al-kashf).

• Zamakhshari, Abu al-Qasim Mahmud bin 'Umar, d. 1140, Al-Kashaf 'an Haqa`iq al-Tanzil: First major rationalist commentary (tafsir bi-r-ra`y), representative of the philosophical Mu`tazila School of Thought. Persian al-Zamakhshari was considered the most outstanding Arabist of his time. His Arabic lexicon remains authoritative.

• Tabarsi, Abu 'Ali Fadl bin Hasan, d. 1143, wrote the first major Qur'an commentary from a Shi'ite viewpoint.

• Razi, Fahr ad-Din Muhammad bin 'Umar bin Husain, d. 1209, Tafsir Kabir: The first major commentary by a Muslim pundit with encyclopedic knowledge, proving the compatibility of the Qur'an with philosophy, astronomy and other natural sciences.

• Baidawi, Nasir ad-Din Abu-l-Khayr 'Abdullah bin 'Umar, d. 1291, Anwar at-Ta'wil: His commentary is still popular because he combines the advantages of both Zamakhshari and Razi without their exaggerations.

• Ibn 'Arabi, Muhy ad-Din, d. 1240, Tafsir al-Qur'an al-Karim: A speculative, esoteric, gnostic and thus heterodox interpretation by the best known Muslim (or Pantheist) mystic (Sufi) of the Middle Ages.

• Ibn Kathir, Abu Wafa Ismail bin Amr, d. 1387, Tafsir al-Qur'an al-'Azim: A verse-by-verse commentary by a historian and hadith-specialist with full chain of transmitters (al-isnad) given for each tradition used. An abridged 30 volume English version is published by Al-Firdaous in London (since 1996)

• The "Jalalain"–Commentary jointly produced by Jalal ad-Din al-Mahalli (d.1459) and Jalal ad-Din as-Suyuti (d. 1505), Tafsir al-Jalalain: Thanks to its compactness it remains popular.

• Abduh, Muhammad, d. 1905, Tafsir al-Manar : This unfinished neo-rationalist commentary in 12 volumes by the late Shaykh al-Azhar in Cairo marks the beginning of the current revitalization of Islam. He criticizes the former preoccupation with lexical and grammatical aspects.

- Qutb, Sayyid, d. 1966, Fi Zil al-Qur'an ("In the Shade of the Qur'an") by the ideological leader of the Egyptian Muslim Brothers during the time of Abd al-Gamal Nassr, executed by him. His 5 volume commentary, written in prison, analyzes Western (and Egyptian) society as neo-heathen and stresses political and sociological aspects.

People interested in a historical survey of the intellectual richness of Arab Qur'an commentaries should consult Mahmud Ayoub's anthology "The Qur'an and its Interpreters".

NON-ARABIC QUR'AN COMMENTARIES

Most of today's 1. 4 billion Muslims do not speak Arabic as their mother tongue. They rely on commentaries of the Qur'an written in their own language of which the following ones are particularly notable:

- Ali, Yusuf, d. 1953, *The Holy Qur'an–Translation and Commentary* (1934): This popular edition by an anglophile Indian Muslim had already seen more than 30 reprints by 1980. Revised versions, eliminating pseudo-rational, theosophic and Christian elements, appeared both in the United States (amana publications, 1989) and Saudi Arabia (Madinah, 1990).
- Mawdudi, Abu-l-'Ala al-, d. 1979, *Tafhim al-Qur'an*: In six volumes, extensively annotated magnum opus of the founder of the Indo-Pakistani reform movement Jama'at-i Islam, in Urdu. An English version by Zafar Ishaq Ansari appears with the Islamic Foundation in Markfield, LE (U.K.).
- Boubakeur, Si Hamza, *Le Coran: Arabic-French*, in two large volumes (1972).
- Asad, Muhammad (alias Leopold Weiss), d. 1992, *The Message of the Qur'an* (1980). As much admired as disputed. Psychologizing rationalist (neo-mu'tazili) translation into Shakespearean English with extraordinarily lucid commentary. Translated into Turkish and Swedish. Beautiful new Qatari version in 2003 (Bitton, Bristol).

- Grimm, Fatima et al., *Die Bedeutung des Qur`ans* (1997): German-Arabic, in five large volumes, prepared by five German and five Arab-born women. Uses commentaries from classical and modern Qur'an exegeses.

Qur'an commentaries can be grouped as follows:

- Traditional (Tabari, Ibn Kathir, Jalalain)
- Sectarian (Muhammad 'Ali and all Shi'i commentaries)
- Mystical (Tustari, Ibn 'Arabi)
- Rationalist (Zamakhshari, Abduh, Asad)
- Apologetic (Yusuf 'Ali)
- Political–Islamist (Mawdudi, Qutb)
- Non-Committal (Grimm)

Sectarian commentators tend to read out of the text what they first put into it.

Rationalists try to explain supra-natural phenomena scientifically. Apologists seek to build bridges to the Christian world view and value system. Islamists are action oriented, treating Islam like an ideology.

In view of this rich variety and plurality of interpretations of one and the same text, one appreciates Annemarie Schimmel`s cheeky remark that a completely clear revelation would not be revelation.

The Qur'an as a Legal Text

No people has ever been civilized more
quickly than the Arabs by the Qur'an.
                    – Muhammad Hamidullah

Shari'ah

The Qur'an is primarily a religious book concerned with theological matters.

However, in as much as Islam is both a faith and a way of life, the Qur'an also addresses legal matters, without thereby becoming a treatise of jurisprudence. The normative elements of the Qur'an are called "shari'ah", originally meaning "road leading to the source". This way water is equated with salvation. These normative elements can be broken down into rules concerning man's relationship with
- God
- his environment (society, animals, nature)
- himself.

These rules may be absolutely binding or in the nature of recommendations, just as prohibitions may be absolute or in the nature of discouragement.

There are rules whose violation will have no legal consequences in this world (fi-d-dunya), others may be punishable in this world and the other (fi-l-akhira).

Muslim rationalists do not agree with Muslim traditionalists about the nature of what is forbidden or evil. Is it bad because God forbade it? Or did God forbid it because it is bad? A dispute without consequences in as much as both sides agree that what is forbidden or commanded is forbidden or commanded.

Muslim lawyers refuse to identify all normative verses of the Qur'an definitely because it is unforeseeable which verses, one day in the future, might become legally relevant. Yet it seems clear that about 600

Qur'anic verses have a normative potential, of which the bulk–some 400 verses–deal with ritual, i.e. matters not considered legal in Western systems of law.

Of definite legal rules in the Qur'an by far the largest number–about 70 verses–concern matters of family and inheritance marriage and divorce, child raising, orphans, intestate and testate succession, compulsory portion of inheritance. These very detailed, even intricate regulations are mostly to be found in surahs 2, 4 and 33.

Ruling on matters of gender relations and sexuality the Qur'an gives detailed instructions as well, even dealing with questions of clothing, hygiene, and etiquette. In the process, moral issues are given legal status.

About 10 verses only address the question of how to run an Islamic State (obligatory consultation; office of president; religious minorities); roughly 80 are devoted to matters of finance and economics (prohibition of speculation, usury, and interest on capital). 25 verses concern defense (international contracts, humanitarian law of war) and civil procedure (law of evidence).

Unexpectedly, only 30 Qur'anic rules concern penal law (murder, injury, robbery, theft, slander, high treason, adultery) and criminal procedure (evidence, statute of limitations).

All this–not only criminal matters–is "shari'ah".

Rules revealed as divine are not subject to human legislation. Consequently, the Qur'anic family and inheritance law–codified or not –is still integrally observed in most Muslims countries, Tunisia and Turkey being exceptions. But the shari'ah, too, must be properly understood through contextual interpretation in order to respond to the conditions of modern industrial societies. Muslim jurisprudence, after all, must give answers to issues like surrogate motherhood, brain death, genetic manipulation, organ transplantation, or cloning.

PRINCIPLES

In addressing contemporary issues Muslim lawyers arrive at conclusions in conformity with the Qur'an even if there are no directly applicable specific Qur'anic rules (an-nass). In their absence solutions can be found through analogy (al-qiyas), i.e. applying rules to facts (merely) similar to the cases regulated by the written law. This can be done most safely if one constantly verifies that analogical rulings are in accordance with the guiding principles of the Qur'an (al-maqasid). As such have been identified justice (al-adl), including equal treatment (ethnical and religious non-discrimination), communal solidarity (seeking the common good), and dignity of the individual.

With the help of these legal instruments Muslim jurisprudence arrived at axioms like the following:
- everything is allowed that has not been expressly forbidden
- dire emergency overrules (to be driven by necessity is no sin: 2: 173)
- punishment must not be disproportionate to the crime committed (42: 40)
- religious law is to make life easier, not more complicated (2: 185; 22: 78)
- common good has preference over self-interest
- if faced with two evils, the lesser one is to be chosen
- what leads to something forbidden is itself forbidden.

The joint application of both analogy and the principles of Islamic law provides Muslim jurisprudence with a remarkable flexibility and adaptability and safeguards its relevance for modernity.

IJTIHAD

To interpret the Qur'an, not only but most notably its legal provisions, is the task of people qualified for it (al-mujtahid). This honorary title is unofficially conferred on specialists who are at home in the Qur'anic sciences, including grammar, pre-Islamic poetry, and the history of revelation. Their models are the founders, called Imams, of the main Muslim schools of jurisprudence, i.e. Abu Hanifa (700-767), Malik b. Anas (716-795), Idris al-Shafi'i (767-820) and Ahmad ibn Hanbal (780-855).

Their humane scientific tolerance should remain exemplary: Each of them was convinced of being right and the others to be wrong. But each one also admitted that he might be wrong and the others right. That explains why invariably they terminated their expositions with wa'llahu 'alam (but God knows better / best).

It is as sensational as it is true that Ibn Shafi'i, the most brilliant theoretician of Muslim jurisprudence, drastically altered his exposition of Islamic law after having moved from 'Iraq to Egypt. The Qur'an was the same, but circumstances were not.

In order to escape sectarianism modern interpreters of the Qur'an should be as liberal as their great predecessors. Their aim should be the gradual development of a new consensus (al-ijma) among the representatives of all legal schools. Instead of their disappearance it is, however, more likely that we shall see the emergence of one more Muslim school of jurisprudence: a European-American School which provides emigrant and Western Muslims with answers to issues which arise first within the secular Occidental techno-civilization.

Strictly speaking the problems facing Muslims in the West are not new. All through history every new generation of Muslims had to appropriate the Qur'an for itself. This Book is not only as inexhaustible as the sea. Like the sea it remains the same while moving and looks new every day.

An experiment will show what is meant: If one reads the entire Qur'an attentively twice within a year, the second time around one will discover aspects totally overlooked during the first reading.

Bible and Qur'an

In essence, the divine Qur'anic message is ecumenical.
— Paul Schwarzenau

The links between Qur'an and Bible are numerous: linguistic, substantive, historical and dogmatic.

DOGMATIC LINKS

The Qur'anic message is so complete and universal that it can stand on its own, well-rounded and closed. But Islam has not been created in isolation.

Nor does it consider itself a a new religion. Rather Muhammad presented Islam as restoration of the monotheism practiced by Abraham, the common religious ancestor of Jews and Christians as well.

In fact, the Qur'an frequently refers to certain parts of the Bible: The Torah (at-tawrat), i.e. the five Books of Moses (Pentateuch), the Psalms (az-zabur) and the Gospel (al-injil):

It is He Who has sent down the Book to you in truth, confirming what came before it. And He sent down the Torah and the Gospel aforetime as a guidance for mankind... (3: 3 f.)

Consequently, both Jews and Christians are qualified in the Qur'an as specially protected "People of the Book" (AL al-kitab):

Say: "Oh, People of the Book, come to an agreement between us and you: that we shall worship none but God... (3: 64)

It is indeed significant that Muslims do not call these religions after the author or collector of their "book".

Accepting, in principle, specific parts of the Old and New Testaments, Jewish and Christian law is valid for Muslims as well, provided it has not been overruled by the Qur'an (2: 106; 13: 39).

LINGUISTIC LINKS

Biblical material in the Qur'an comes with Hebrew vocabulary called "Israiliyat". This was a puzzle for people for whom the entire Qur'an was "in clear Arabic language" as confirmed by 12: 2 and 16: 103. Imam al-Shafi'i (767-820) in his Risala (Chapter IV) solved the problem by treating the Israiliyat as borrowed and Arabized words.

It was more difficult to prevent Jewish and Christian notions from semantically sneaking into Qur'an interpretations, aided by seemingly synonymous vocabulary. This was almost unavoidable with concepts like Logos, Spirit (ar-ruh) and Covenant. Christians automatically associate "Logos" with Christ Incarnate and Spirit with the third divine person within their concept of Trinity. Likewise Jewish people quite naturally associate "Covenant" with the idea of Israel as a Chosen People that entered into a privileged, mutually binding contractual relationship with God (Exodus 34, 27).

Muslims, on the other hand, neither personalize "Spirit" nor "Logos" when encountering *ruh al-amin* (loyal spirit) or *ruh al-qudus* (holy spirit), as in 26: 193; 16: 102 and 17: 85. In these cases they rather think of divine inspiration. "Covenant" they see as God's acceptance of (unilateral) promises made by the tribes of Israel.

SUBSTANTIAL LINKS

In as much as Islam aspires to restore Abraham's pristine monotheism, it is intimately linked to Judaism. In the Qur'an Jewish prophets figure prominently, including Aaron, Abraham, David, Elias, Elisha, Ezra, Ishmael, Jacob, Jesus, Jethro, Job, Jonah, Joseph, Lot, Moses, Noah and Solomon. Altogether 23 Israeli and two Arab Prophets, Hud and Muhammad, appear in the Qur'an. Six of its surahs are even named after prophets, i.e. Abraham (14), 'Imran (3), Hud (11), Jonah (10), Joseph (12), and Noah (71).

Moses is mentioned in the Qur'an 136 times, Abraham 69 times and Jesus ('Isa) 26 times; in addition, references to him are made as "Messiah" and "Son of Mary". It may seem extraordinary but in the

Qur'an Mary appears more frequently than in the New Testament; the 19th Surah (Maryam) carries her name.

It should be noted that the Qur'an is silent on a number of weighty Jewish prophets like Amos, Ezekiel, Habakuk, Isaiah, Jeremiah and Malachi.

Given that the Qur'an is so intimately interrelated with the Bible one should not be surprised when finding similarities between the two. It would, however, be wrong to conclude that the Qur'an borrowed Judeo-Christian material, not to speak of plagiarism. Some tendentious Orientalists contend indeed that the Qur'an included misunderstood heterodox material of sectarian–Samaritan, Nestorian and Coptic–origin.

The history of the Qur'an, known in all detail, excludes plagiarism. At any rate, logic tells us that two similar texts may, or may not, have a common source. Also one should be alert to the fact that Biblical stories play entirely different roles in Bible and Qur'an. The Bible is narrative. The history of the Jewish people and its prophets is told in great detail. The Old Testament in particular paints historic portraits of epic scale and even records repulsive, sinful behavior of prophets like David (2 Sam. 11, 2-26).

In contrast, the Qur'an presupposes that its readers are familiar with those events. The Qur'an is rather preoccupied with drawing quintessential moral conclusions from Biblical material. When referring to it the Qur'an is not historical and concrete but archetypical and abstract. In the Qur'an, Biblical narratives are turned into ahistorical, eternally instructive episodes. In this way, the Qur'an according to Jacques Berque "de-mythologized" the Bible.

As far as Jesus is concerned, the Qur'an is interested only in his nature and role, not his life in greater detail.

To put an end to this discussion: Where Biblical and Qur'anic narratives differ both may be right.

CONTRADICTIONS

This is not to say that there are no real, irreconcilable discrepancies between Bible and Qur'an. Listed here are nine:

1. The Bible refers to God as "Father" (Arabic: ar-rabb). The Qur'an never does, because the concept of father implies gender and procreation. Instead in the Qur'an God appears as Creator . None of the Muslims` "99 most beautiful names" or properties of God (al-asma al-husna) are gender related.

2. According to the Bible, on the 7th day God "rested" from creating the universe (Genesis 2, 2 f.; Exodus 20, 11; 31, 17). In contrast to this anthropomorphic concept the Qur'an leaves no doubt that God never slumbers nor sleeps nor tires (2: 255; 50: 38).

3. It is amusing to read that the world according to the Hebrew calender was created some 5765 years ago. The Qur'an does not pronounce itself on such details of astronomy.

4. Far-reaching are the conflicts between the Biblical and the Qur'anic descriptions of what happened in Paradise:

(a) According to the Bible, Adam and Eve were forbidden to eat from the Tree of Knowledge because otherwise they would learn to distinguish between good and evil (Genesis 3, 5, 22). The Qur'an makes clear that man should indeed learn to distinguish between good and evil, calling itself guiding standard and mark of distinction (al-furqan; 2: 53, 185; 3: 4; 25: 1). In fact, the Qur'an leaves open why the tree in question was forbidden (7: 19), its prohibition merely being a test of discipline and obedience. It was Satan alone who insinuated that Adam and Eve were kept from obtaining angelic nature and immortality (7: 20; 20: 120).

(b) According to the Bible Eve tempted Adam into sin. She took the first bite from the forbidden fruit (Genesis 3, 1, 7, 12). Adam accused her of that. St. Paul, however, used this as a pretext for demonizing woman as such (2 Kor. 11, 3; 1 Tim. 2, 14). This trend had tragic consequences in Christian history, in particular the burning of two million European (and some American) women as "witches".

The Qur'an relates the same happening grammatically using the dual number (dualis), thereby indicating that Adam and Eve had acted jointly. Their fall resulted from a joint-venture.

(c) According to the Bible, the fall of Adam and Eve meant punishment for mankind as a whole. Adam and Eve were thrown out of Paradise, unforgiven. Theirs was the original, the hereditary sin (Gen. 3, 16 f.). This fatal concept of collective guilt made people cry out for salvation, look (and find) a savior, and interpret Jesus` death as "sacrificial" and "salvatory" (Romans 5, 13-19).

In contrast, the Qur'an–like Jesus (Matth. 19, 14)–teaches that children are born sinless and therefore in no need of baptism (39: 70). Adam and Eve had forfeited Paradise (7: 24 f.), yes, but God had forgiven them (2: 37; 20: 122). The Qur'an indeed restates repeatedly that nobody is to answer for somebody else`s sins (17: 15; 52: 21).

5. According to the Bible, the Children of Israel are a "Chosen People" whose God is a jealous God (Exodus 34, 14; 1 Samuel 25, 32), the God of Israel (and therefore, for gentiles, not necessarily the only god). In contrast to this qualified monotheism God in the Qur'an presents Himself as "the Lord of mankind , the King of mankind, the God of mankind" (114: 1-3). As "Lord of the Universe" (1: 2) He is everybody`s God.

6. Before Moses the rulers of Egypt were "kings", not yet "pharaohs". Nevertheless, the Bible refers to all Egyptian rulers as "pharaohs" (Exodus 40, 2, 13, 17 f., 22). Arabs of the 7th century knew no better. It is therefore remarkable that the Qur'an neatly distinguishes between the "king" of Egypt at the time of Joseph (12: 43, 50, 54) and "pharaoh" at Moses` time (2: 49 f., 44: 17, 31).

7. According to the Bible Noah was a drunkard (Genesis 9, 20), Abraham and Isaak were caught lying (Genesis 12, 10 ff.; 26, 1 ff.), Moses was a brutal conqueror (Deuteronomy 3, 6 ff.), David a tyrant, adulterer and murderer (2 Samuel 3, 12, 16; 11, 2-26), Solomon a tyrant, womanizer and even apostate (1 Kings 2, 13 ff.; 11, 1-9), and Lot committed incest while drunk (Genesis 19, 31 ff.). In contrast the Qur'an proceeds from the assumptions that all real prophets while not being sinless by definition lead exemplary lives.

196 ISLAM AND QUR'AN: AN INTRODUCTION

8. The Qur'an while not necessarily excluding crucifixion as such denies Jesus' death on the cross (4: 157).

9. The Qur'an alerts to the fact that God manifested Himself not only in holy scripture or–as Christians believe–in Jesus but also in the entire universe. Such religious naturalism is foreign to the Bible. The notions of Incarnation and Trinity, i.e. of the divinity of Jesus, were not included in this list of discrepancies because there is no scriptural basis for either doctrine. The list as it is is long enough to explain why Muslims do not accept the Bible as such as trustworthy (2: 174f).

(f.) To be on the safe side, Muslims rely on the Qur'an to such an extent that the Bible plays no significant role for them. This reductionist approach has Qur'anic support:

- Muhammad was the last prophet, sealing all preceding prophecy (33: 40);
- God left out nothing of importance in the Qur'an (6: 38);
- God's religion was completed by the Qur'an (5: 3, 5th sentence, and 48).

Thus Muslims deal with the Bible much as Catholics deal with the Old Testament. It is not coherent, at any rate, if Muslims after rejecting the Bible in principle base their arguments on parts of it. This usually happens with respect to Deuteronomy (18, 15 and 18) and John (14, 26 and 16, 13) when read as forecasting Muhammad.

THE QUR'AN AND SCIENCE

God's Work cannot contradict God's Word
– Sayid Ahmed Khan

SCIENTIFIC COMPETENCE ?

The Qur'an never stops urging Muslims to observe nature as signs (ayat') of His. This is usually followed by appeals to ponder these observations. At the same time the Qur'an is realistic in stating that perceiving God in the signs of nature is an act of *faith* that precedes mere observation. In other words, an irreligious mind will not find God, even in nature.

Be that as it may, Muslims saw themselves encouraged by the Qur'an to study God in His works, and to do so not *deductively*, like the Greeks, but inductively, i.e. *empirically*. The results were stunning. From the 8th to the 15th centuries, Muslims became leading scientists in mathematics, physics, biology, zoology, chemistry, optics, astronomy, medicine, geography, historiography, agriculture, and military sciences.

Contemporary Muslims are still so proud of these achievements that they risk becoming victims of their nostalgia for the Golden Era of Abbasid Baghdad and Umayyad Cordoba. Others risk to go astray for mistaking the Qur'an as a natural sciences textbook or even an encyclopedia.

This being said, Muslims can be proud of the fact that there is not a single Qur'anic statement about nature and the universe which ran afoul of modern sciences. In fact, none of the many historical and scientific errors of the Bible were repeated in the Qur'an.

Maurice Bucaille ("The Bible, the Qur'an and Science") already in 1976 drew attention to this remarkable situation.

To give a few examples: In contrast to the Bible the Qur'an teaches that the universe–and with it time and space–was created instantaneously (Big Bang ?). What seems like stages of development had all been programmed from the beginning. God had called all being into existence by saying:

Be! And it is (kun fa jakun). And:
**Those who disbelieve, do they not see that the skys and
the earth were one single mass that We split, and that We
created all living things from water ?** (21: 30). And:
**Then He turned to the sky when it was still smoke
and told heaven and earth: "Come** [into being]..." (41: 11)

That there should be several heavens, i.e. galaxies, was beyond the imagination of 7th century Arabs, nor would they have believed that they, too, developed from water (21: 30; 24: 45).

Modern astronomy also seems to confirm that the universe is constantly expanding; the Big Crunch theory is gaining ground. On that the Qur'an has this to say:

We have built the sky with (Our) **power, and look
how We expand it** (steadily) (51: 47).

Truly sensational is the Qur'anic description of the human fertilizing process, starting with a drop of sperm (16: 4) that clings to the womb. At a time when procreation still was surrounded by superstition and magic the Qur'an indicated that the human embryo results from embedding sperm in the womb.

Even more sensational, this was the subject of the very first Qur'anic revelation (96: 1f.): **Recite, in the name of your Lord Who created - created man from something that clings** (min ʿalaq).

It took 1300 years for the Muslims to understand this first revelation, thanks to the microscope now available.

Astonishing, too, is the Qur'anic statement concerning the pharaoh who pursued Moses and his tribe to the Red Sea and drowned there. In 10: 92 it was predicted that his body would not decay. The body of the pharaoh in question–Minephta / Mernephta, son of Ramses II–in 1898 was found mummified in the Valley of the Kings near Thebes.

It is legitimate to study the compatibility of Qur'an and science, provided one does not slide into rationalistic apologetics. Alas, some Muslims are virtually screening the Qur'anic text for scientific pearls.

This accounts for the disturbing assertions that 23 verses are devoted to natural science (Alami Mohamed M'Chich), dealing with outer space research (55: 33, 35), the exploits of astronauts (6: 125), the contraction of the universe (11: 107 f.), deep sea research (24: 40), destruction of the environment (30: 41), and–oh wonder–microphysics (34: 3). Some, like Rashid Rida, had even convinced themsel-ves that the Qur'an dealt with electricity and microbes. . .

In most cases it can be shown that the pretended natural science aspects of the Qur'an are due to the so-called Easter Egg Syndrome: One finds in a text exactly what, via projection, one had put into it oneself.

In some, rare cases, however, the Qur'an seems to combine state-ments on natural science with theological ones. 34: 3 is a case in point:

He is the Knower of the unseen. Not an atom's weight, or less than that or greater, escapes Him in the heavens and on earth...

The crucial Qur'anic concept of "atom" (adh-dharrah) had already been used in that meaning by pre-Socratic philosophers, and is still used by modern nuclear physicists. So one has the choice of understanding 34: 4 as a description of God's Omniscience, an acknowledgement of the molecular, atomic and sub-atomic structure, or both.

ORACLES ?

The Qur'an is future oriented in as much as it focuses on man as a mere transit passenger in this world, on his final destination in the world beyond. In great conformity with Christian ideas, Islamic eschatology depicts future events in considerable detail–Last Judgement, Paradise and Hell.

This aside, in 30: 2-4 the Qur'an made a number of historical predictions that came true: The Persians had driven the Byzantines out of Damascus in 613 and out of Jerusalem in 614. It looked as if they were there to stay, indefinitely. Yet the Qur'an said: **The Romans have been defeated in the near land. But after their defeat they will be victorious within three to nine years** (30: 2-4).

In 622, *eight* years later, entirely unexpectedly the Byzantines were able to crush the Persians.

Nevertheless, the Qur'an is not to be mistaken as a collection of oracles.

Islam strictly forbids engaging in soothsaying (5: 90), surely also for predictions supposedly based on the Qur'an itself.

Science and the Qur'an

Currently, world-wide, the Qur'an is
the ideologically most influential text.
                              – Toby Lester, 1999

Ever since John of Damascus (d. about 750) Christian theologians tried to dismantle and defeat the Qur'an, being scandalized by it. Most of them made no sincere effort to comprehend this irritating text but to fight it polemically.

This was true for the Abbot of Cluny, Peter the Venerable (d. 1156) as much as it was true for Martin Luther (d. 1546) and Philipp Melanchthon (d. 1560) in spite of their inadvertent contribution to the spreading in Latin of the Qur'anic text.

Essentially this picture did not change, at least not for some time, when the Qur'an made its first appearances in European languages. Pioneers were André du Ryer with his French translation, "L`Alcoran de Mohamet" (Paris 1647), Alexander Ross with his English translation, "The Alcoran of Mahomet" (London 1648), Solomon Schweigger with his German translation, "Alcoranus Mahumeticus, das ist: der Türcken Alcoran, Religion und Aberglauben" (Nuremberg 1616) and Claude Etienne Savary`s alternative French translation, "Le Coran" (Paris 1783).

A true Qur'anic science, useful for Muslims as well, only developed with, and after, Silvestre de Sacy (d.1838). Now large biographies of Muhammad appeared as well, like those by Gustav Weil (1834) and William Muir (1861). Orientalist interest in the dating not only of each surah but each verse within each surah turned into an obsession, culminating with Theodor Nöldeke`s prize-winning "*Geschichte [History] des Qorans*" (1860). It was for him to introduce the now current periodization. His book was the most important individual piece of Orientalist research of his century.

The 19th century was of course renowned for its imperialistic stance.

Within Orientalism this found expression, e.g., in Gustav Flügel's Arabic publication of the Qur'an, in 1834, with a verse numbering of his own making (Corani texti Arabicus). Thank God, in the post-modern world it would be politically incorrect to deal that way with somebody else's holy script. In a way, all the later assaults against the Qur'an began with Flügel. Richard Bell, supposedly following scientific criteria, in 1937-1939 in Edinburgh, published a "rearranged" version of the Qur'an, for Muslims an arrogant act of blasphemy. Worse yet, in the middle of the 20th century Arthur Jeffery together with some German Orientalists like Otto Pretzl attempted to assemble a new "critical" text of the Qur'an, based on some 40.000 snippets of Qur'anic fragments. Few people were sorry to see this project go up in flames during a bomber attack on Munich in World War II.

But even this attempt could be topped. Modern attempts of deconstruction reached a new zenith with John Wansborough and his team at the London School of Oriental and African Studies. His book " Qur'anic Studies: Sources and Methods of Scriptural Interpretation" (1977) turned out to be the starting shot for extremists like Michael Cook ("Hagarism: The Making of the Islamic World") and Patricia Crone. To the delight of Israel these ideologues tried to prove that Islam was a late, 9th century invention. They claimed that

- the Qur'an had not existed before the end of the 7th century, i.e. not during the time of the Prophet;
- Mecca had never been a center of the Muslim world;
- the Arab conquests preceded Islam;
- the flight of the Prophet (al-hijra) never took place;
- early Muslims had not called themselves "Muslim".

They arrived at these absurd conclusions by excluding all Muslim sources for the writing of Muslim history. This is like writing about Judaism without the Bible and about Christianity without the New Testament. Indeed, already Ignaz Goldziher had responded to such pseudo-scientific escapades by asking: "What would be left over of the Gospels if one were to apply to them the critical methods applied to the Qur'an?" The question is in fact: What is more important—method or truth?

The Wansborough school has been scientifically discredited. No single Western faculty of Islamology is taking it seriously. So why should Muslims?

Of course, American, British, French and Dutch Orientalists of the 19th and 20th century willy-nilly played a role in the imperialist ploys of their countries.

Also they could hardly help being children of their agnostic/atheist age and its secularist paradigms. Not believing in the existence of God, how could they do justice to a text that claims to be a divine revelation? They naturally tried to de-mythologize the Qur'an the way it had already been done with the Bible by Christians themselves, like Rudolf Bultmann in Protestantism. Parvez Mansoor was therefore right when commenting upon the Orientalist relationship with the Qur'an: Rarely, if ever, the sacred script of a world religion has been treated with so much "pathological animosity".

Fortunately, lately numerous Orientalists emerged who realize that rationally alone one cannot cope with the phenomenon of revelation because the numinous has its own (religious) rationality. Notably Islamologues like Angelika Neuwirth ("Studien zur Komposition der mekkanischen Suren", 1981) and Neal Robinson ("Discovering the Qur'an", 1996) are making major attempts not just to dissect but to *understand* the Qur'an. (In the process, Robinson became Muslim.)

As compared with the 19th and much of the 20th century, Orientalism now is less interested in linguistic and historical aspects of Islam, focusing rather on its anthropological, sociological and political facets.

In short: The Qur'an is alive and well, surviving all scientific assaults with flying colors.

THE QUR'AN AND THE ARTS

Monotheism was not only an intellectual feat.
It also required a change of consciousness.

– Karen Armstrong

CALLIGRAPHY

Thinking of Islamic art means thinking of calligraphy. And people when thinking of calligraphy usually do not have beautiful Chinese or Japanese penmanship in mind but artful Arabic texts. Indeed, calligraphy is not only the most outstanding branch of Islamic art but a climax in the world history of art.

That this craft developed so well in the Islamic world in two ways is deeply related to its religion. Firstly, the Muslim veneration of the Qur'anic text calls for utmost care and embellishment in its writing. Secondly, Islam discourages representative art, thereby encouraging abstraction. Therefore, in a way, Muslim calligraphy can be seen as aesthetic compensation for the ideological repression of concrete painting in Islam. Of course Arabic lends itself to decorative manipulation since it allows both horizontal and vertical writing and uses isolated letters, unconnected to the right and the left, apt to float in a calligraphed space. Finally, the diacritical signs of Arabic script are so detached that they can respond to the *horror vacui* of Islamic art. In short, Arabic is a supremely decorative medium.

During the 7th century the Qur'an was recorded in *Kufi* script which, however, had not been invented in Kufa but rather in Jordan. The angular Kufic script remained in use up to the 12th century. Its stiff and austere letters were written on the line only. Verses were not numbered individually. Rather groups of verses were set off with rosettas. (The verse numbering later undertaken in Basra, Kufa and al-Madinah did not fully match.)

Business required a script which could be written fast and flexibly. This gave rise to the second great Arabic form of script, called *Naksh*. As from the 12th century it replaced Kufi, even for writing the Qur'an. This elegant script with its mathematical proportions was developed in Baghdad by the Abbasid Wasir Ibn al-Muqla (d. 940).

All other scripts of Arabic are children of these two, *Kufi* and *Naksh*. They include *Tuluth*, for the first time permitting diagonal writing, and *Ruq`a*, basis of today's Arabic handwriting.

The Maghrib region in North Africa and Muslim Andalusia saw the growth of the flowery, highly dynamic *Maghribi* script with its delicate semi-circles.

A leaf written in Maghribi, busy and therefore hard to read, looks like a beautifully balanced forest of abstract vegetation.

Other peaks were reached with *Nasta'liq* in Safawid Iran where, for the first time, written lines began to hang through; and with *Diwani* in Ottoman Turkey, invented by Hafiz Osman (d. 1689). Now one arranged texts in such a way that they formed images, for instance of birds or ships. Thus the first verse of Surah al-Fil (The Elephant) could be written in elephant shape.

The Qur'an-Museum (Bait al-Qur'an) in Bahrain gives an overview over all these types of Arabic script.

From the earliest times, Muslims decorated their homes with quotations from Qur'an and Sunnah, calligraphically written. Preference is for texts with golden letters stitched on black velvet because they recall the cloth covering the Ka'aba in Mecca. Favorite texts are the Basmala written in a circle, the 112th Surah, and the Prophetic saying "God is beautiful and loves Beauty".

In execution, Muslim calligraphers take such licenses that it is nearly impossible to decipher their lettered creations.

Today, the Qur'an is written by hand only as a model for printing. Hard to believe: The first time ever, the Qur'an was printed in Hamburg, Germany, in 1694, and not in a Muslim country. In fact, the now standard printed version of the Qur'an had to await the end of World War I (King Fu`ad edition, Cairo).

But printed versions, too, can display splendidly illuminated pages. Especially excellent in this respect are editions of the Dar al-Fajr al-Islami in Damascus and the Mushaf al-Madinah, bound in green and gold, produced by the King Fahd ibn 'Abd al-Aziz Qur'an Printing Shop in al-Madinah.

Founded in 1984, with an annual capacity of 10 million copies, it has already printed close to 200 million copies of the Qur'an, in 24 languages. None of them are sold. All are given away.

ARCHITECTURE

During a lecture in Berlin, I heard Oleg Grabar say that "Islamic art are artifacts which show, or could show, inscriptions in Arabic." Since he teaches Islamic art at Harvard, this perplexing definition carries weight. How amazing–and how telling–to define an art form by its decoration, i.e. calligraphy.

Grabar`s definition sounds reductionist, even defeatist. But in the end, after having seen great Islamic art from India, Afghanistan and Usbekistan to Iran, Turkey and Egypt and from Tunisia and Morocco to Andalusia, one cannot but agree with him: Islamic art, profane or sacred, is held together by friezes, i.e. decorative bands of Arabic calligraphy.

From this perspective one should take another look at exciting architecture like the Bibi Khanom Mosque in Samarkand, the Shah Sultan Husein Madrasa in Isfahan, the Blue Mosque in Tabriz, the Dome of the Rock in al-Quds (Jerusalem), the Büyük Karatay school in Konya or the Grand Mosque in Cordoba. All these buildings bear significant Arabic inscriptions, inside and outside, frequently in form of multicolor tiles covering domes or prayer niches (al-mihrab).

Only into rugs Qur'anic texts are never woven, since one steps on them.

RECITATION

In December 609 CE the Qur'anic revelation began with the command: Iqra! (96: 1) which means both "Read!" and "Recite!" In fact, the Qur'an is less a book to be read silently than a text to be proclaimed. Only then it reveals all of its beauty.

At-tajwid, the Arabic equivalent of psalmody, was already practiced in the 7th century CE. Even then there were commonly accepted rules for accentuation, assimilation, reading pace, and pausing. To recite the Qur'an artfully and with a beautiful, pleading voice turned into an art form (at-taghanni).

Nowadays as well famous Qur'an reciters compete with each other. Some of them issued the entire Qur'an on tape or compact discs, like Shaykh 'Ali 'Abdallah Shabir (19 cassettes) and Shaykh 'Abd al-Basit 'Abd as-Samad (44 cassettes). In 1989 the Kingdom of Morocco issued the Qur'an on 20 cassettes, recited by Muhammad al-Kantawi. More recently, an Arabic-English version, produced by Shaykh Sultan al-Qasimi of the Emirate of Sharjah became available. Shaykh 'Abdul Bari Muhamad recites the Arabic and Gai Eaton the English text as translated by Marmaduke Pickthall.

The Qur'an contains rules for its own recitation. According to 73: 4 recitation should be measured and clear, without haste (75: 16) and in "easy portions" (73: 20). The aim is to present the text in a manner both dignified and intelligible (at-tartil), without musical accompaniment or show effects. This is best achieved with vibrating tenor voices betraying emotion. Reciters must not take any liberties vis-à-vis text, pronunciation or accentuation. For the Prophet the most God-fearing reciter was the best.

The Muslim East maintains the style of recitation (al-qira`at) formalized by Hafs b. Sulayman al-Kufi (d. 796). A chain of two links only connected his tradition with the caliphs 'Uthman and 'Ali. The Muslim West follows the style of recitation formalized by Nafi'. Five other traditional ways of reciting (al-huruf; sing. al-harf) are canonically admitted.

These "seven readings" (al-qira'at as-saba') fully honor the text of the Qur'an and its meaning. They differ only in pronunciation, melody, and rhythm. One should know that the Qur'an had been revealed mostly in the dialect of the Qur`aish in Mecca. When Islam spread to other tribes–Asad, Kinana, Tamim–all over the Arab peninsula, the

Prophet tolerated their way of pronouncing, in line with their own dialects, in order to facilitate their learning of the Qur'an.

Thanks to research conducted by Yasin Dutton we now know that the colored dots found in early Kufi versions of the Qur'an may have helped notating different forms of recitation. He believes that dots in red signify the normal way, while green and yellow dots mark alternative readings.

In greater detail the differences between various "readings" can be summed up as follows:

- Pronunciation: Differences in emphasis and agglutination ("m" may be pronounced as "n" or "l"). End consonants may receive more resonance through adding a shade of "e" Thus one recites **"Qul huwa Allahu ahade "** (112: 1).
- Timing and Tempo: introducing pauses, lengthening letters.
- Melody: florid arabesques
- Pitch: high, whining voice.

Qur'an recitation has become an art so highly formalized that Qur'an recitation competitions are held in most Muslim countries and, internationally, in Malaysia. Time and again, it is students from non-Arabo-phone countries like Indonesia or India who win.

Thanks to the Qur'an and the art of its recitation high Arabic (al-fusha) is now understood, if not spoken, from the Arab Gulf to the coast of Mauritania.

Thanks to this book alone, Arabic is the only language which for more than 1300 years preserved its relevance, vocabulary, grammar, and sound as a lingua franca . In contrast, no Englishman, Frenchman or German can read or even understand the English, French and German of only half a millennium ago. The Qur'an is indeed the only book that remains unchanged and yet immediately usable for any Arab speaker, and that for 1300 years.

DEALING WITH THE QUR'AN

> The Qur'an is a guide for all living beings on the planet
> earth, a textbook for learning a new language–the language
> of spirituality.
> – Muzaffar Haleem, (*The Sun Rises in the West*, 1999)

EVERYDAY LIFE

According to 'A'isha, the Prophet's intelligent wife, he had turned into a walking Qur'an: "The Qur'an was his nature." It is therefore logical that devout Muslims try to *incorporate* the Qur'an as much as possible into their thinking and speaking. No matter what is discussed, they will inject relevant Qur'anic verses, introduced by *qala ta'ala* (the most Supreme said). This goes to prove that the Qur'an is the very center of Islam (Annemarie Schimmel).

Muslims speak of *al-Qur'an al-karim* (the noble Qur'an) or *al-Qur'an al-hakim* (the wise Qur'an), just as they refer to Mecca as *al-Makka al-mukarrama* (the blessed one) and to al-Madinah as *al-Madinah al-munawwara* (the enlightened one).

In fact, the Qur'an is still treated with the reverence which once had been reserved for the Bible in the West. In many Muslim households a copy of the Qur'an is the only book. At any rate, it will be kept in an honorific place, be it a precious casket, the highest shelf of the bookcase, above the entrance door or hanging above the conjugal bed.

Muslims are fond of presenting copies of the Qur'an, as a gift. They will not sell copies, at any rate not above the production costs. Saudi Arabia each year gives 10 million copies of the Qur'an away. Every Mecca pilgrim can expect to receive one.

Reverence for the Qur'an requires that one touches it only when ritually pure, i.e. in the state required for prayer (56: 79). Also, one will never throw away a copy of the Qur'an, nor individual leaves of it.

For reading the Book one may use a foldable wooden stand (ar-rihla). One only starts reading after pronouncing the Basmala and saying *'audhu bi-'llah min ash-shaytani-r-rajim* (I take refuge with God from the accursed Satan).

Reaching certain passages in the Qur'an, like 7: 206 and 96: 19, in accordance with them one is required to prostrate. (These passages are indicated on the margins of the Qur'anic text by the word *sajda*, i.e. prostration). And one terminates reading in the Qur'an by saying *sadaqa'llahu-l-'adhim* (God the most High spoke true), kissing the book upon closing its pages.

In Muslim countries Qur'an recitations have assumed a *ceremonial* function in public. Every conference or gathering is opened with a few verses of the Qur'an. This borders on the *ritualistic* use of the Qur'an when, in miniaturized form, it is carried on the body as talisman or amulet. As golden pendants attached to necklaces the "protective surahs" al-Falaq and an-Nas (113, 114) are especially popular. It definitely is ritualistic abuse when the Qur'an is written so small that it fits on a single page or comes as tiny booklets in 3x2,5 cm format, readable only with a magnifying glass.

With such *bibliolatry* one is about to use the Qur'an *superstitiously*. The first such case happened during the protracted battle of Siffin (657 CE) when the 4th caliph, 'Ali b. Abi Talib was confronted by the Umayyad counter-caliph Mu'awiyya. His troops attached leaves of the Qur'an to their lances, thereby awing their opponents into an armistice, fateful for them. Here the Qur'an had been reduced to a *fetish*.

Today, *profanization* of the Qur'an is the more dangerous trend. Since its recitation is available on cassettes and CDs one is exposed to it even in Muslim owned taxis from New York to Delhi. Loudspeakers are turned on so high that the noise (!) of the Qur'an can drown out the noise of big city traffic. On top of it, taxi passengers continue their conversation without paying any attention to what is recited. *Haram!*

QUR'ANIC SCHOOLS

One may be a Christian without knowing by heart even a single phrase of the Bible. For Muslims this is unthinkable because they must be in command of several small surahs in order to be able to pray. In each prayer unit (ar-raka´) of each of the five prayers to be performed daily, as a minimum the 1st Surah al-Fatiha has to be recited (compulsory exercise). In each prayer, some units are to be complemented by other surahs, or parts of them (free exercise). These have to be learned by heart because the Muslim way of praying excludes the use of prayer books.

From the very beginning of Islam, many Muslims have been committing to memory the entire text of the Qur'an (al-huffaz; sing. al-hafiz). At any time of Islamic history hundreds of thousands of Muslims knew the Qur'an by heart.

This explains, e.g., the specific Muslim capability of resistance against political suppression, recently proven once more in Albania, China and the Soviet Union. Islam simply cannot be eliminated by confiscating the copies of the Qur'an since it remains stored in many a memory.

In 1999 I visited a Qur'anic school in Wad Madani, between the Blue and the White Nile in Sudan. In this place, for 375 years the Qur'an has been taught the same way. Today, children come here from all over Black Africa, "adopted" by their Shaykh for the six years of their studies. Many begin at the age of eight; quite a few of them are blind. They begin learning a new passage of the Qur'an every morning at 2 o`clock when it is still cool. After the morning prayer and breakfast, the students start writing down this new passage on wooden tablets, with washable ink. After this has been checked by their teacher, the students rehearse the Qur'anic passage they had learned the day before. By now it it close to noon-time. Time for prayer, lunch, and a long nap.

I was encouraged to ask students to recite specific passages of the Qur'an.

With amazing speed and accuracy, each one asked delivered.

In such *hafiz*-factories one teaches the Qur'an exclusively because if the Sunnah were added there would be danger of confusion.

All the students in Wad Madani are arabophone.

There are, however, Qur'anic schools as well for students who are not. This is for instance the case with institutions in the M`Zab region of Southern Algeria (Ghardaia, Beni Izguen, Malika, El-Ateuf) whose population is Berber speaking. Their kids learn the Qur'an without understanding Arabic, with double justification:

First, it is meritorious to learn God's Word regardless of the degree of understanding it. (Who can claim to understand it ?) Second, young brains can learn the Qur'an by heart in an amazingly short time. Later on there is always a chance to learn the meaning of what is solidly committed to memory.

This being said: In the language of the Qur'an "memory" and "warning" (al-dhikr) are synonyms. Stuff for pondering.

LITERATURE

I. QUR'AN TRANSLATIONS INTO ENGLISH

Asad, Muhammad, *The Message of the Qur'an*, Bitton, Bristol 2003

Bewley, Abdalhaqq and Aisha, *The Noble Qur'an*, Norwich 1999

Pickthall, Marmaduke, *The Glorious Qur'an* (many editions since 1930)

'Ali, 'Abdullah Yusuf, *The Meaning of the Holy Qur'an* (many editions)

II. BOOKS

Ansari, Muhammad Abdul Haq Ansari, *Learning the Language of the Qur'an*, Aligarh 1997

Ayoub, Mahmoud, *The Qur'an and its Interpreters*, Albany, N.Y. 1984, 1992

Azami, M. M., *The History of the Qur'anic Text*, Leicester 2003

Cragg, Kenneth, *The Event of the Qur'an*, London 1971

Dutton, Yassin, Red Dots, Green Dots..., *Journal of Qur'anic Studies*, Vol. 1, No. 1, London 1999, pp. 115 ff.

Hammad, Ahmad Zaki, *The Opening to the Qur'an*, Bridgeview, Illinois 1996

Haleem, Muhammad Abdel, *Understanding the Qur'an*, London 1999

Imam, Ahmad 'Ali al, *Variant Readings of the Qur'an*, Herndon, Va. 1998

Jan, Tarik, *The Life and Times of Muhammad Rasul Allah*, Islamabad 1999

Khadduri, Majid, *al-Shafi'i`s Risala*, Cambridge 1987

Lings, Martin, *The Qur'anic Art of Calligraphy and Illumination*, New York 1987

Nadim, Abu-l-Faraj, *The Fihrist*, New York, N.Y. 1970

O.I.C., IRCICA, *World Bibliography of Translations of the Qur'an 1515-1980* (with supplement), Istanbul 1986

Osman, Fathi, *Concepts of the Quran*, Los Angeles 1997

Robinson, Neal, *Discovering the Qur'an*, London 1996

Sells, Michael, *Approaching the Qur'an*, Ashland, Oregon, 1999

Surty, Muhammad Ibrahim, *The Science of Reciting the Qur'an*, Leicester 1987

Tabari, Abu Djafar al-, *The Commentary of the Qur'an*, Oxford 1987 ff.

CHRONOLOGICAL SEQUENCE

MECCAN SURAHS

1: 96	23: 53	45: 20	67: 51
2: 68	24: 80	46: 56	68: 88
3: 73	25: 97	47: 26	69: 18
4: 73	26: 91	48: 27	70: 16
5: 1	27: 85	49: 28	71: 71
6: 111	28: 95	50: 17	72: 14
7: 81	29: 106	51: 10	73: 21
8: 87	30: 101	52: 11	74: 23
9: 92	31: 75	53: 12	75: 32
10: 89	32: 104	54: 15	76: 52
11: 93	33: 77	55: 6	77: 67
12: 94	34: 50	56: 37	78: 69
13: 103	35: 90	57:31	79:70
14: 100	36: 86	58: 34	80: 78
15: 108	37: 54	59: 39	81: 72
16: 102	38: 38	60: 40	82: 82
17: 107	39: 7	61: 41	83: 84
18: 109	40: 72	62: 42	84: 30
19: 105	41: 36	63: 43	85: 29
20: 113	42: 25	64: 44	86: 83
22: 112	44: 19	66: 64	

MADINAN SURAHS

87: 2	94: 57	101: 59	108: 64
88: 8	95: 47	102: 24	109: 61
89: 3	96: 13	103: 22	110: 62
90: 33	97: 55	104: 63	111: 48
91: 60	98: 76	105: 58	112: 5
92: 4	99: 65	106: 49	113: 9
93: 99	100: 98	107: 66	114: 110